GRAVEL PIT FISHING

By the same author

COARSE FISHING ILLUSTRATED
(with Keith Linsell)

TREVOR HOUSBY

Gravel Pit Fishing

HERBERT JENKINS
LONDON

First published 1968 by
Herbert Jenkins Ltd
2 Clement's Inn, London, WC2

SBN 257 66697 4

PRINTED IN GREAT BRITAIN BY
NORTHUMBERLAND PRESS LIMITED
GATESHEAD

CONTENTS

To Carol

1

INTRODUCTION

Household and industrial pollution has now ruined many of our rivers, and, despite constant work by river board authorities, the annual pollution rate seems to increase rather than diminish. Couple this problem with the constant expansion of building projects and the outlook as far as the angler is concerned looks rather bleak. Fortunately, to cope with the ever-increasing demand for building materials, many man-made lakes have been created by the sand and gravel companies. These large, often featureless, waters now provide anglers all over the country with first-class coarse fishing. Man-made pits vary considerably in size and depth depending on how much overburden has to be removed to expose the seams of gravel sand or other raw materials. A good many pits are filled in as soon as they become finished, but others are left unfilled to provide the coarse fisherman with good sport. One go-ahead sand and gravel firm has even opened its own angling scheme, the object being to make good fishing available to the many anglers who are unable to join angling clubs. This particular firm makes every effort to make its pits attractive by landscaping the ground round the perimeter of the pits and by leaving islands in the pits themselves.

There can be little doubt that many disused gravel pits contain fish of record size, for a great many specimen fish are caught each year by pit fishermen. The record tench, for example, came from a pit in Huntingdonshire, and pike, perch, bream and eels of record size are thought to exist in various pits all over the country. Whether or not a record carp will ever be caught from a pit remains to be seen, but there are several pits in the home counties which contain carp in excess of 30 lb., some of which have been only stocked with carp during the past ten years. In one such pit in the Darenth Valley the fish reached a weight of 18 lb. in five years. A water of this calibre is more than capable of providing carp of over 40 lb. in weight if given the opportunity to do so. Once a pit becomes disused and the particles of suspended silt settle, the water soon clears and becomes rich in weed and insect life. These clear-water pits offer the best fishing, for, although sport is often rather slow, the average fish from such a water is usually extremely large.

Angling clubs often obtain the fishing rights of man-made pits and providing they plan their restocking programmes carefully they can assume that their members are provided with consistently good fishing. A badly planned restocking programme, however, leads to a poorly-balanced fishery, and indiscriminate restocking with the wrong types of fish can only lead to trouble. Bream and tench make good stock fish, but it is no good stocking a water with a mixture of both, for both fish feed in a similar fashion on similar food and will naturally compete with each other to such an extent that they will quickly exhaust the food supply of a pit, and without adequate nourishment neither species will grow to any size. Bream, of course, provide all-the-season-round sport whereas tench are only really a summer species. Carp and bream seldom mix well, but carp and tench live happily together; roach and rudd should only be introduced sparingly into a water for both have a tendency to breed rapidly and overrun a pit. Perch make good stock fish for, providing they are placed into a clear water pit which is rich in food, they will grow to a large size. Pike also thrive in pits, and a well-balanced water should contain a reasonable head of perch and pike to keep the other species under natural control. Many other species of fish find their way into gravel pits via feeder streams on other inlets. Basically, however, roach, rudd, bream, tench, carp, pike, perch and eels are best suited to life in these man-made waters.

Pits present a problem to the newcomer, for their large average size and featureless appearance make it difficult to decide where to begin fishing. Contrary to a popular belief, the bottom of a pit is seldom flat or of a uniform depth and it pays to spend a day or two plumbing depths and making a map showing the likely spots for fishing. A plumbing expedition will quickly show just how much variation in depth there can be in a pit, and my experience has shown that most pit beds are made up of a series of deep gullies or runs between areas of shallower water. Fish of all types use these gullies like roadways, and a bait cast so that it falls into such a run will usually catch fish. Many anglers refuse to be bothered with making a preliminary investigation of this type and after a series of blank or semi-blank expeditions give up pit fishing entirely. With the right approach, however, gravel pits can yield magnificent catches to the thoughtful, patient angler. 'Chuck and chance it' techniques are seldom productive, for pits often require special techniques if fish are to be caught consistently. I have fished gravel pits for the last fifteen years and have been fortunate enough to catch many specimen fish from these waters, my best pit fish being as follows: carp $17\frac{1}{2}$ lb., pike 22 lb. (six over 20), perch 3 lb., tench 5 lb., roach 2 lb. 8 oz., rudd 2 lb. 6 oz., bream 7 lb., trout $5\frac{1}{4}$ lb., eels $5\frac{1}{4}$ lb., chub $4\frac{1}{4}$ lb., plus many other fish of specimen size.

Man-made pits are the waters of the future, for with an ever-expanding population and a demand for more houses, many more pits will be developed. These in years to come will provide first-class sport to future generations of anglers, providing, of course, that these waters are carefully preserved and nurtured by knowledgeable anglers. This book is intended to show just how pit fish can be caught. Obviously, new techniques are always being evolved; most of these are simple variations on the techniques described in this book, and as it is impossible to describe every single tackle set up in common use the ones described are those that are basically used by knowledgeable all-round fishermen and specimen hunters. These basic tactics have been used to catch hundreds if not thousands of specimen fish all over the country and are well tried and tested methods which can be relied upon to catch fish consistently; the inquiring angler will no doubt improve upon these methods to meet with conditions in the pits which he fishes, but for a start the methods described in the following chapters will catch fish in any water under most conditions.

2

BREAM

Bream anglers usually talk of their catches in terms of stones or even hundredweights of fish, and because of this bream have a reputation for being stupid sheep-like creatures which can be caught one after the other. To some extent this is true, for when a big shoal of hungry bream is located it is often quite possible to catch fish after fish in quick succession. These huge shoals usually consist of fish between 2 and 4 lb. in weight, and bream of this size tend to be incautious feeders; but the really big bream are a far different proposition, for not only are they cautious in the extreme but as they only feed in very small shoals it is almost impossible to catch large quantities of specimen bream at one sitting. Occasionally a few very big bream are taken in a large catch of average-sized fish. This probably happens because two distinct shoals have become temporarily mixed, but does not prove that bream of all sizes can normally be found in the same shoal, for bream definitely seem to shoal according to size.

Bream, like many fish, thrive in gravel pits, and many clubs deliberately restock these waters with bream, knowing full well that these fish will provide extremely good sport in years to come. There are many pits which are famous for bream fishing, and some of them contain bream fast approaching 10 lb. in weight.

There are two types of bream in Great Britain: these are the common or bronze bream and the silver bream. This latter fish, which has a very limited distribution and a very low weight, is of little interest to most anglers. The record silver bream weighed 4 lb. 8 oz. but this was an exceptional fish, for most silver bream weigh less than 1 lb. Few anglers deliberately fish for silver bream, and those that are caught are usually taken accidentally on baits intended for other fish. The common or bronze bream, however, is an extremely popular fish with most anglers. Its wide distribution and comparatively high average size is undoubtedly the main reason for its popularity, for being common in most areas it is within reach of many anglers, and because of its size it gives everyone the opportunity of catching reasonably big fish. By general standards, bream of 3 or 4 lb. are average fish, a 5-pounder is a good one, and any bream over 6 lb. in weight a specimen. Although the common bream record stands at 13 lb. 8 oz., very few anglers ever manage to catch a bream of over 7 lb. in weight; during most years, one or two bream between 9 and 11 lb. are reported to the Angling Press. A good many gravel pits are known to hold bream of this size, but these fish are rarely caught, although they are sometimes hooked and manage to break away before being brought within reach of the landing net.

Probably one reason why big bream are rarely caught is that they tend to feed mainly at night, when most anglers have packed up and gone home. There is now in this country a Bream Catchers' Club whose members devote the bulk of their fishing time to the problems of catching monster bream, and already members of this organisation have taken bream close to 10 lb. in weight. Most of the really big bream caught in this country during the last ten years have been taken by night anglers, fishing large still waters of the gravel pit type. Big bream catching, like most forms of specimen hunting, consists of many long hours of concentrated effort for very few bites. This sort of fishing does not appeal to the majority of anglers but it is necessary if big fish are to be caught consistently, and big bream are no exception to the rule.

Through the efforts of a number of eminent anglers, we know a great deal about the movements and feeding habits of many species of fish, but until recently bream fishing has to a large extent been neglected, and because of this comparatively little is known about the life and habits of these fish. Big bream fishing, however, is becoming increasingly popular, and already several new and effective techniques have been developed specifically for bream fishing. These tactics are already producing results, and no doubt in future years more and more big bream will be taken because of these developments.

LOCATION OF BREAM

Fish location is one of the major problems that faces the gravel-pit bream angler, for, unless the pit in question is over-run with bream, the individual shoals can be extremely difficult to track down. Usually gravel pits which hold vast numbers of bream are unlikely to produce any worth-while specimens for bream have huge appetites and if thousands upon thousands of bream are continually competing for food it does not take long for the natural food supply to become exhausted. Consequently the average size of bream taken from a water of this type is extremely low. Because of this it is advisable deliberately to seek out gravel pits which hold a limited stock of bream, for these waters are the ones most likely to produce bream of specimen size. The overstocked waters, of course, can and will produce large aggregate weights of fish and can usually be relied upon to fish well under most conditions, but for big fish the understocked pits make the best venues.

To some extent, bream are an obliging species, for on hot, still evenings when the water temperatures are high they will give themselves away by rolling and priming on the surface. Many specialist bream anglers consider this act to be a prelude to feeding; whether or not this is an accurate belief it is difficult to say, but by fishing close to a spot where bream have been observed rolling, it is often possible to catch large quantities of these fish. By careful scrutiny, it is also possible to get a rough idea of the individual size of the fish that are likely to be caught from the swim, for bream shoals are usually made up of fish of equal size. Consequently, if fish of an estimated 3 to 4 lb. are sighted then it is probable that the bulk of the fish caught from that swim are likely to be of a similar size. Personal observation leads me to believe that as the fish get larger, the size of the shoal decreases, until finally just a handful of 6-, 8- or 10-pounders are left from a shoal which originally contained a hundred of more 1 or 2 lb. specimens. Obviously many of these original fish die off over the years, and finally the shoal consists of a nucleus of top-quality fish, which continue to grow until they reach the peak of their maturity. Because of this it always pays to make a careful note of any really outsize bream seen rolling, and to fish the swim where the fish were sighted to the exclusion of all other swims.

During the early weeks of the season, large numbers of bream often move into areas of shallow water to cleanse themselves after spawning. Few anglers, however, bother to fish the shallow sections of a pit, and this is a mistake, for it is pointless to fish a nice comfortable swim, which has a good depth of water if the fish are at the other end of the pit splashing about in the shallows. Later as the season progresses and the bream recover from their spawning activities, the shoals will forsake the shallow water and gradually work back into the deeper swims. But for the first week or two after the season opens the shallows are the places to fish, for that is where the bream are most likely to be. This is particularly true when the weather is warm and settled, for bream, like so many fish, delight in shallow sun-warmed water.

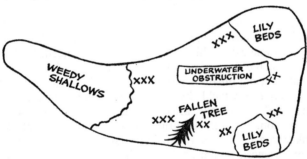

1. Rough map of bream water showing weeds, snags, etc.
X = Bream caught.

Having once located a water which holds a few shoals of very big bream, and decided to fish it consistently, it is a good idea to map thoroughly the pit in question, carefully marking out each swim from which bream have been caught and sighted and each weed bed, ledge, hole or snag as it is located (see fig. 1). By doing this job properly it is possible gradually to build up an accurate picture of the water, and, more important still, of the movement of the bream shoals that it contains. It may well take several seasons to piece together a map of this type but it is well worth the effort, for by using it in conjunction with any physical or mental notes made, on prevailing water temperatures, climatic conditions, or times of year when fish have been caught, it is often possible to locate feeding bream shoals on each visit. Naturally a project of this kind takes time, but it is time well spent, and in the long run will simplify the location problem considerably.

During the winter months bream, like tench and carp, have a tendency to hibernate. On a mild, bright winter day, however, they sometimes awake briefly and may well feed rather spasmodically for an hour or two, usually during the middle part of the day when the light is brightest. To make contact at all with gravel-pit bream during the winter months, it is advisable to fish in the deepest sections of the pit. Winter bream fishing is at best a chancy proposition and for every good day when fish are caught many blank days will be recorded.

TACKLE FOR BREAM

Bream have a reputation for being poor fighters, and because of this many anglers use extremely light tackle for bream fishing. To some extent this reputation is well founded, for bream seldom make long, fast runs when hooked; but make no mistake—a big bream is more than capable of smashing comparatively heavy tackle by its sheer bulk and doggedness. The extreme depth of the bream's side makes it an awkward proposition, for once it turns and makes off parallel to the bank it can be extremely difficult to stop and turn, and many an experienced bream angler has had his tackle smashed by bream which have made off in this fashion. There is nothing dashing in a bream's struggle to shed the hook, but at the same time a big bream can put up quite an awe-inspiring battle, particularly when hooked in very deep water, and for this reason it pays to use fairly substantial tackle for all aspects of bream fishing. Remember also that when a big shoal of these fish are encountered, the tackle may also have to withstand hour after hour of continuous hard work, and ultra-light gear cannot be expected to take punishment of this type for any great length of time.

Rods

In years gone by, bream rods were huge heavy instruments

made of lancewood and whole cane. Now most bream specialists rely on 11 or 12 ft. rods, manufactured of split cane or, better still, hollow glass. The split-cane rods have the nicest action but even the best split-cane rods quickly become permanently distorted and warped when used for bream fishing. Hollow glass, on the other hand, takes far more punishment without losing shape and nowadays most experienced bream fishermen purchase hollow-glass rods with an easy progressive action. Glass match-type rods that only bend for the last 18 in. of their length should be avoided, for these have neither the power nor the action required to set a hook at any distance or to control a bream of any respectable size. These rods are quite suitable for roach fishing or match work on rivers but should have no place in the gravel-pit angler's equipment. There are many highly suitable rods available and any good tackle shop should be able to display a range of these rods. The ideal bream rod has a test curve of approximately $1\frac{1}{4}$ lb. This will handle lines of 4 to 7 lb. b.s. comfortably and will be suitable for all aspects of basic bream fishing.

Reels

Most gravel pits are large and, during the daytime at least, the bream shoals have a tendency to feed at some distance from the bank. For this reason centre-pin reels can seldom be used comfortably. A medium-sized fixed-spool reel, however, is ideal, and by carrying two or three spare spools, each loaded with a different strength of line, it is a simple enough operation to switch tackle several times during the course of a day as circumstances dictate.

Lines

It is inadvisable to fish with a line much under 4 lb.'s breaking strain where big bream are concerned, for the sheer bulk of the fish can break the line on the strike, and a big bream hooked in deep water can apply a considerable amount of pressure. Fortunately most gravel pits are comparatively snag free. Some of the very old pits, however, may contain dense weed beds. In this case it is advisable to use a 6 or 7 lb. b.s.

line when fishing in close proximity to surface or sunken weed beds. That extra couple of pounds b.s. can make all the difference between landing or losing fish among the weed stems or fronds. Monofil line is ideal since, being cheap, it can be changed regularly throughout the season, for continuous bream catching soon weakens even the best of lines.

Hooks

Size of hook depends basically on the size of bait, and it is advisable to carry a range of hooks from size four to size twelve for bream fishing. The smaller hooks are used in conjunction with small worm, maggot or cereal baits, the larger hooks for bunches of redworms, lobworms, large lumps of bread paste or crust. Barbed shanked hooks (see fig. 2) are useful for worm baits, for the barbs help to hold the worm in position during casting. When the bream are really 'on', it is advisable to check the hook point at frequent intervals, for once a hook becomes blunt it may cost you a big fish.

2. Barbel shank hook for worm baits.

FEEDING HABITS

Basically the bream is a bottom-feeding fish which seldom rises to the middle or upper water levels in search of food. Consequently most bream anglers fish on or very close to the bottom. This is particularly true of still-water bream, for in slow-moving rivers match anglers often catch large numbers of small bream by trotting a bait slowly downstream. There are, of course, no hard and fast rules in angling, and many a good still-water bream has taken a bait fished well off the bottom, but these instances are definitely exceptions to the general behaviour of feeding bream and can only be classed as 'flukes.'

Almost any edible object will be quickly engulfed by hungry bream, although the main food of these fish consists of minute aquatic insects or the larvae of many free-flying insects which start life in water. Bloodworms are a constant source of food for bream, and in pits where fresh-water mussels abound these too form an important part of the larger bream's food chain. There is also some evidence that big bream have a predatory streak, for during most seasons reports reach the Angling Press of bream which have been hooked fairly inside the mouth on artificial lures intended for pike or perch. Big bream have also been known to pick up small deadbaits, and one well-known Norfolk angler once described to me how he hooked a huge 9 lb. bream on a livebait intended for pike. On the continent, particularly in the Netherlands, tiny artificial baits are commonly used to take bream and roach-bream hybrids. Medium and large bream also make a considerable nuisance of themselves by taking the huge baits used by carp anglers, and more than one 7 or 8 lb. bream has managed to engulf a large, nicely cooked potato bait, which had been prepared by a devout carp specialist to try and overcome the problem of bream tampering with carp baits. For this reason, bream have developed a bad reputation with many dedicated carp anglers, and a number of noted carp fishermen have made their dislike of bream publicly known through the medium of the Angling Press. I can understand this outlook, for I too have been troubled by bream while carp fishing but have long since learned to live with this problem and make the most of it.

A large shoal of hungry bream can eat vast quantities of food, and, because of this, bream fishermen often employ huge quantities of groundbait to attract and hold the attention of any feeding bream shoal which happens to pass within casting distance of the bank. There is much to be said for and against groundbaiting on a large scale, and later in this chapter I would like to go into the groundbait question thoroughly.

BAITS FOR BREAM

Although bream have voracious appetites, they can some-times be extremely fussy in their choice of food, and a bait that caught fish on one outing may produce very poor results on the next, so it is advisable to make a point of carrying a selection of baits on all bream fishing expeditions. Worms, bread and maggots are all good bream catchers, and probably account for more bream per season than any other baits.

Worm is probably the best all-round bait to use, for, being natural, the bream tend to accept it without question. Unfortunately, worms also attract other types of fish as well, and small eels, perch or rudd can often make a thorough nuisance of themselves by snapping up worm-baited tackle long before the bream have a chance to find it. Luckily many gravel pits are devoid of these little fish, and it is on these waters that worms come into their own. Almost any worm can be used as bream bait, but redworms or lobworms are best. Redworms can be used either singly or in bunches of three or four. These bunched worm baits are very effective where large bream are concerned, and often bring about the downfall of a real specimen. Presumably the bream see a ball of wildly wriggling redworms as a mass of enlarged bloodworms and take them accordingly. Lobworms can be used whole or can be broken in half. The tail end of a big lobworm makes a very effective bream bait. Where possible it is advisable to avoid hooking a worm bait too many times for this spoils the natural appearance of the bait. Unfortunately worms are rather soft, and where long-casting techniques have to be employed to reach the feeding bream shoal, it is often essential to hook a worm two or three times to ensure that it does not tear off the hook during casting. Even so it need only be hooked through the head section of its body, leaving a good length of tail hanging freely (see fig. 3).

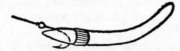

3. Worm hooked through head only leaving tail free to attract fish.

Various types of bread baits are extremely popular with bream anglers, for bread is easy to obtain, clean to use, and highly attractive to bream of all sizes. Bread paste, flake and crust are all effective bream baits, and can be used with confidence on most waters that hold bream. On a clean bottom, which is devoid of blanket weed or really soft mud, bread paste is a favourite bait. Unfortunately it is heavy in comparison to other bread baits and will quickly sink from sight into the soft weed or ooze of a mucky-bottomed swim. Flake, on the other hand, is ideal, for, being fairly light, it will sink slowly and come to rest gently on top of the weed or mud. This is an important point to remember and it pays to find out as much as possible about the bottom of each bream swim you locate, for details of this kind can make the difference between success and failure. Bread crust fished on leger or float tackle can also be used to combat the problem of bottom weed, for the crust, being buoyant, will rise as far as the trace between hook and weight will allow, and remain suspended on or just above the blanket of weed.

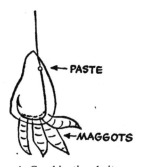

4. Combination bait.

At one time grains of stewed wheat were a popular and widely used bream bait, but nowadays few anglers bother to obtain or prepare this cereal. Bream of all sizes can be caught on maggots either used singly or in large bunches. Once again however, small fish can make a nuisance of themselves by gorging maggot baits before the bream have a chance to get to them. Combination baits of maggot and bread flake or paste (see fig. 4) are good for bream, and can be relied upon to take fish on days when the bream fail to respond to more conventional baits.

Big baits for big fish is a policy which pays off where bream of specimen size are concerned, for big bream, like so many fish, are lazy creatures which prefer one large mouthful to a lot of small ones. For this reason it is advisable to use generous portions of bait on large hooks. This applies particularly to waters which are known to hold very large bream.

Groundbait

Veteran bream anglers talk in terms of hundredweights where groundbait is concerned, and few specialist bream anglers use less than 30 or 40 lb. of groundbait in a single session. This may sound a fantastic amount of groundbait to the average angler, but a shoal of bream is capable of clearing up a vast amount of food in a remarkably short space of time,

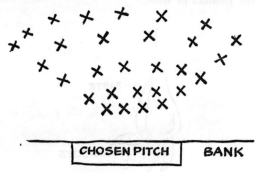

5. Groundbaiting pattern to be used for bream fishing.

and once they have exhausted the food potential of a swim, they will quickly move on to fresh pastures. Consequently it takes a considerable quantity of groundbait to attract the attention of a bream shoal and almost as much again to hold the fish in the swim for a whole day's fishing.

Breadcrumbs, sausage, rusk and pigmeal can all be used for groundbait, and household scraps of bread and cooked potato peelings can be added to give extra attraction to the basic ingredients. Many anglers make the mistake of adding too much water to their bream groundbait, so that it breaks up as it hits the surface of the water. This is wrong, for to be effective the groundbait should sink rapidly to the bottom in one lump and then break up gradually. In this way a thick carpet of groundbait can be laid along the bottom. Great care should be taken to throw the groundbait out fanwise so that the swim is thoroughly baited (see fig. 5). By doing this correctly the bream shoal can be held in the swim for a long period of time. If the groundbait is all deposited in one small area, however, the fish will clear it up far too quickly.

Having once been attracted to a swim, bream can often be held for long periods of time, by throwing out fresh quantities of groundbait at regular intervals throughout the day or night, whichever the case may be. Although heavy groundbaiting is an essential part of general bream fishing, it can be a disadvantage where really big bream are concerned, for very big bream live and feed in very small shoals, and too much groundbait can easily over-feed a shoal which only contains six or eight fish. So on waters where bream are few and far between, but of a large average size, it is advisable to restrict the quantity of groundbait used.

Samples of the hook bait can be added to the groundbait mixture, chopped worms, maggots and lumps of bread paste all add to the attraction of the basic groundbait, and will in no way distract the bream away from the baited tackle.

METHODS OF CATCHING BREAM

Float fishing

In swims of moderate depth, float tackle can be used quite effectively to catch bream. It is rare, however, for float fishermen to catch very large bream, for these fish usually fall to leger tackle. As the bream is a bottom feeder, the laying-on technique as described in the Roach chapter is the only really practical method of float fishing. This can be a most pleasurable way of taking bream, for bream bites on float tackle are easy to see and nearly always follow a set pattern. Normally the first indication that a bream has found the bait comes when the float bobs sharply two or three times. After these preliminary knocks, the float usually lifts up and keels over as the bream picks up the bait and lifts the shot from the bottom (see fig. 6). As a rule the float will tip right up and lay

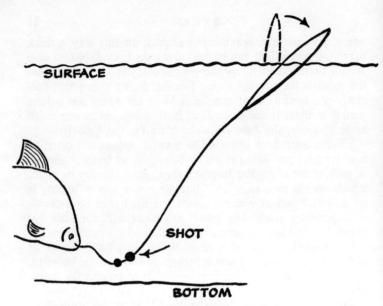

SURFACE

SHOT

BOTTOM

6. Float keels over as bream takes bait and lifts shot from the pit bottom.

flat before sliding gently off over the surface, gradually submerging as it does. The strike should be made only when the float is moving off in this fashion.

Float fishing is only recommended for sport; most anglers wishing to catch extra-large bream will be well advised to rely on leger tackle.

Legering

Being almost entirely a bottom-feeding fish, bream respond well to baits presented on leger tackle. This is fortunate, for in deep pits, float fishing even with a sliding float can be an extremely awkward technique to employ. The leger, however, is simple to set up, easy to cast, and extremely sensitive in operation, which makes it an ideal terminal rig to use in deep-water swims. For general bream fishing a plain free-sliding leger (see fig. 7) can be used with confidence, but when the bream are in a finicky mood and refuse to take a bait presented on standard leger tackle, a far more sensitive set of terminal tackle should be employed. The link leger (see fig. 8) is ideal, for with the lead on a separate length of nylon a fish can pick up a bait and move quite a long way without feeling the

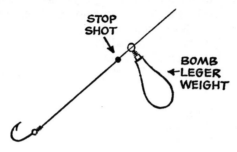

7. Standard running leger.

weight of the lead at all. Because of this, bites on link-leger tackle are often firm, decisive affairs which are extremely easy to strike at. The distance between lead and hook depends a

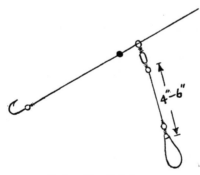

8. Sensitive link leger.

great deal on personal preference and experiment. On a new water, 18 in. between hook and lead or hook and lead link is about right, to start with. This can then be adjusted to suit conditions as they exist in the water in question.

Soluble leger weights

Carp fishermen have been using floatless weightless tackle for years, and to some extent this tackle can be adapted for use against gravel-pit bream. It does not, however, work very well in deep water, for some form of weight is essential to sink the bait rapidly to the bottom and also as an aid to casting; for a big bream bait is small in comparison to an average carp bait, and in consequence is not heavy enough to cast any

9. A: Soluble leger weight. B: Link swivel.

distance without a further weight of some kind being used. A simple and effective way of adding weight and yet fishing with a free line is to use a soluble weight. Sugar cubes or roughly shaped salt blocks fall into this category, and a supply of these should be prepared at home. Basically this preparation simply consists of tying a length of cotton round the sugar or salt cube leaving a projecting loop (see fig. 9a), then when the tackle is made up a small link swivel should be run on to the line and stopped by a tiny dust shot 6 or 8 in. from the hook (see fig. 9b). The link on this swivel can then be clipped on to the cotton loop attached to the soluble weight. The bait can then be placed on to the hook and the cast made. The weight will last long enough to sink the bait, but will dissolve after a few minutes' soaking, leaving the tackle devoid of any extra unnecessary weights, the dust shot and swivel being far too light and small to alarm any taking fish.

The credit for this idea should go to the specimen-hunting fraternity of this country, who continually work on new pro-

jects that might help them to catch big fish. This soluble
weight idea is one of the most successful experiments yet
made.

The swim feeder leger

Bream respond well to many forms of groundbaiting, but
at times, when the fish are behaving very cautiously, a standard
swim feeder (see fig. 10) can be extremely useful as a means of
attracting fish to the vicinity of the bait. Originally the swim
feeder, which consists simply of a perforated plastic cylinder
to which a lead strip of the required weight has been added,
was designed for use in rivers, the idea being to stop one end
of the 'feeder' with predampened groundbait, fill the centre
section up with loose samples of the hook bait, before finally
stopping the remaining section with a second portion of damp
groundbait. The whole thing could then be cast out leger
fashion, and after a few minutes' immersion, the action of the
water would gradually cause a steady stream of groundbait to
wash downstream over the baited hook. Fish following this
trail upstream naturally locate the bait and take it confidently.

Obviously a flow of water is required before a swim feeder
loaded in this fashion can function correctly, and therefore
few gravel pit or still-water fishermen include a swim feeder
in their basic kit. By using dry groundbait in the centre section
of the feeder, however, it is possible to make a first-class bait
bomb which will explode after several minutes of immersion
and fill the water around the bait with a mass of floating food
particles which attract but do not actually feed the fish. There
is nothing complicated about this idea, although it is advisable
to use as much dry groundbait as possible, so that when the

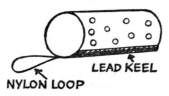

10. Swim feeder.

water penetrates and causes the dry bait to expand, the resulting 'explosion' is as large as possible. In deep, clear water, the exploding swim feeder can be highly effective.

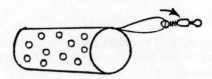

11. Swivel added to nylon loop.

Shop-bought swim feeders are supplied with a simple nylon loop attachment (see fig. 11). This can be improved greatly by adding a small swivel which will allow the feeder to slide freely on the line like a standard leger weight. Swim feeders can, of course, be made up at home from thin gauge plastic or polythene sheet. The colour of the material used does not matter, for it is advisable to always paint swim feeders with matt green or olive paint. By making one's own swim feeders it is possible to adapt them up to suit one's own requirements. To ensure that the feeder will remain free-running at all times, it is a good idea to incorporate two small buttons into the design (see fig. 12). These can be mounted on top of the feeder by two short lengths of wire. By running the line through the uppermost holes of these buttons, a very free-sliding feeder can be obtained. It is, of course, essential to trim off any protruding wire ends, as these may catch up round the reel line during casting and spoil the action of the feeder entirely. For gravel pits, swim feeders should be made on the small

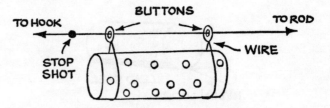

12. Swim feeder with buttons added.

side. Over-large feeders, although capable of holding far more groundbait, may alarm fish and cause them to go off feed or move to another part of the pit. Used sensibly and at the right time a swim feeder can be an asset to the serious bream angler; used badly and without thought it can only be a drawback.

Swing tip and target

Various top-notch match anglers are continually trying to perfect methods of bite detection which will allow them to catch the maximum quantity of fish in the shortest possible amount of time. One item of tackle which was developed for this purpose has proved its worth so conclusively that it deserves a place in any keen angler's tackle box. I am, of course, referring to the swing tip (see fig. 13), which was designed specifically for detecting the gentlest of bream bites.

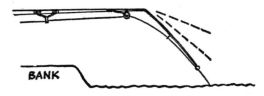

13. Swing tip in action, dotted lines indicate movement on tip as bites are registered.

Although primarily designed for bream fishing, the swing tip can also be used while roach, rudd or tench fishing. The swing tip is simply a flexible extension which clips on to the rod tip. It carries several conventional rod swings through which the line runs in the normal way. When a swing tip is used the rod should be set parallel to the bank; this is essential both from the bite-detection point of view and also for the shelter provided by the bank itself. The strike should be made parallel to the bank so that the line is pulled through the water. An upward strike causes a delay due to water pressure and may lead to lost fish. The rod tip should only be raised when a fish is actually hooked.

Match anglers have experimented a great deal with terminal tackle to be used in conjunction with the swing tip. This research has shown that a certain type of link leger gives the best results. This leger is made up as follows: first take a 6 or 8 in. length of 7 or 8 lb. b.s. nylon, tie a 3/16th diameter split ring to one end and a swivelled bomb of suitable size to the other. The reel line should then be passed through the split ring, the hook being tied directly to the end of the reel line. A stop shot is then nipped on to the line and the tackle is ready for use. The distance between stop shot and hook depends upon the prevailing mood of the fish. A 2 ft. trail is most useful, but the shot can be moved up or down the line as required. Once the tackle has been cast out, the line must be tightened so that the swing tip hangs down forming an angle (see fig. 13) between rod tip and leger weight. The slightest pull will then be clearly indicated by the tip moving upwards. If the taking fish moves in towards the bank, the tip will drop downwards.

Swing tips are highly sensitive indicators which are unfortunately affected by the slightest breeze. Because of this it is essential to fish in a sheltered position whenever possible, otherwise many bites may pass unnoticed. The swing tip was originally developed for use on slow-flowing waterways but is perfectly adaptable for still-water use, particularly for bream, which often bite very shyly. Match anglers are, of course, more interested in quantity, not quality, but the swing tip can be used most successfully to take bream of specimen size. I was once fortunate enough to take nine bream between $4\frac{1}{2}$ and $5\frac{3}{4}$ lb. while swing-tipping on a large pit near Sevenoaks in Kent. During this session I missed only one bite, although the fish were taking the baits very gently. Swing-tipping over a long period of time can be a tiring occupation, for the tip must be watched at all times, otherwise bites may be missed completely. Constant practice is required to perfect the technique of swing-tipping, but once this method has been fully mastered it can be most productive.

Many match anglers are now using a special target cum windshield for use with the swing tip. These targets are made of a square of transparent perspex, which is attached to a single foot made of wood or metal (see fig. 14a). In use, this foot is driven firmly into the bank so that the target rests snugly on the ground. In shallow water the target can be set actually in the water so that the lower edge is submerged. It is essential to make sure that there is no gap left along the bottom edge of the target, otherwise the wind passing through this gap may cause the otherwise sheltered swing tip to sway about which will make accurate bite-detection impossible. In use, the rod tip should project over the target so that the angled

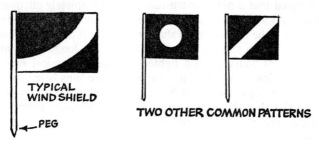

14. A: Typical wind shield. B and C: Two other common patterns.

swing tip hangs down on the opposite side of the target to the angler. The transparent target should be painted black, leaving only a window through which the swing tip can be watched. Many anglers now paint complex designs on their targets. This is all right for match fishing, but the average angler out for a day's sport can use a simplified version of the match anglers' shield without fear of missing bites. The pattern most widely used has a diagonal window (see fig. 14c) but a target with a round or half-circular window can also be used (see fig. 14b).

Butt indicators

Butt indicators work on a similar principle to the swing tip, except that they are clipped to the butt section of the rod. If the line is tightened the indicator can be angled in the same way as a swing tip, and will show a bite by moving up towards the rod or dropping back towards the reel, depending on which direction the fish moves as it takes the bait. Although useful, these indicators are inferior to the true swing tip.

Thoughts on rods for use with the swing tip

Swing-tip experts seldom agree on the question of what length of rod to use with the swing-tip extension. Some prefer the longer rods, while other equally successful anglers are convinced that a nine- or ten-foot rod is completely adequate. In many ways it is a matter of personal choice which length of rod is to be used, but the shorter rods are probably the best, for they have a slightly stiffer action than the longer rods, and are also, of course, much lighter. The only practical reel to use for swing-tipping is a fixed spool, centre pins being totally useless for this method of fishing. Most good tackle shops stock swing tips, but they can also be made up at home from long plastic knitting needles and light-gauge, small-diameter polythene tube (see fig. 15).

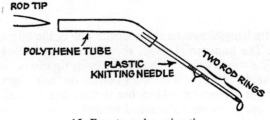

15. Easy to make swing tip.

Bite detection at night

Bream seem to show little fear of artificial light, providing that it is directed across and not into the water. Because of this some bream anglers habitually float fish throughout the night, using a powerful electric torch to illuminate the float. A plain white bird-quill float is normally used for this style of fishing and bites are easily detectable. Although an indirect light does not seem to alarm bream, it is still rather unnatural, and many big bream specialists prefer to fish entirely without a light of this kind, preferring to rely on visible or audible bite indicators.

As bream are bottom feeders there can be nothing to be gained from using a float if it cannot be seen, so leger tackle is the most effective terminal tackle to employ. There are a great many bite indicators in common use. These range from plain twisted silver-paper indicators through to the commercially-made buzzer indicators primarily designed for carp fishing. A good night-fishing indicator should be sensitive, and, more important still, easy to see from any angle. This does not matter if a buzzer is used, but comparatively few anglers other than carp fishermen own an audible indicator. They are, however, an invaluable asset to the regular night fisherman.

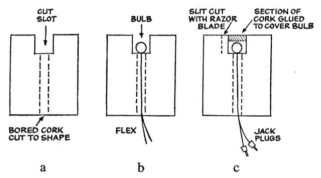

16. How to make a useful illuminated bite indicator.

An extremely simple yet highly affective 'bobbin' type indicator can be made up at home very cheaply from the following materials: a large bottle cork, 12 watt bulb, a yard of hearing-aid flex, two small jack plugs and a grid-bias battery. The cork should be cut and bored (see fig. 16a). Then the bulb should be soldered to the flex. The free end of the flex should then be threaded through the bored section of the cork and the bulb bedded neatly down into the gap. A section of cork should then be fitted into the remaining aperture above the bulb and glued firmly into place (see fig. 16b). When this operation is complete, only the tip of the bulb should be showing, and for added protection it is advisable to make certain that this is countersunk, otherwise the bulb may easily be broken either in use or in transit. Finally a slit should be made in the cork with a razor blade (see fig. 16c) and the jack plugs attached. The indicator is then ready to be plugged into the battery when required. By moving the jack plugs from one battery socket to another it is possible to control the light output to suit one's own requirements. In practice, only a slight glow is needed, for a bright light may cause eye strain. In use, the line should be clipped into the slit on the top of the cork so that the bulb faces back along the rod towards the reel. Providing the line between rod tip and lead is tight, the slightest mouthings of a hungry fish will cause the indicator to rise in a series of jerks (see fig. 17). With an ordinary silver-paper indicator many of

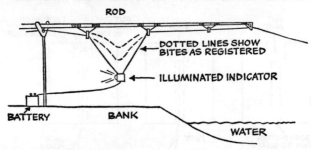

17. Battery attached to illuminated indicator.

these preliminary 'knocks' would go unnoticed, but with an illuminated indicator the slightest pull on the line is clearly visible. Always make the indicator as light and as compact as possible, for a heavy cumbersome indicator will alarm a taking fish and cause it to eject the bait.

When using a bite indicator of this type it is advisable to use only one rod, for it is almost impossible to watch two indicators properly throughout the night. With audible indicators this problem does not arise and two rods can be used comfortably. Bream seldom pick up a bait and make off holding it in their lips as carp do; instead they seem to pick the bait up and drop it two or three times before finally taking it. Consequently bream bites on leger tackle seem to follow a rather set pattern. First the indicator will twitch up and down several times, then finally it will move steadily up towards the rod. Then and only then should the strike be made. A premature strike will usually result in a complete miss, and where big fish are concerned one cannot afford to make too many mistakes of this kind. With a visible indicator every move of the fish can be carefully calculated, but with an audible indicator it is very difficult to judge just what is going on and then it is advisable to sit back and wait for a run to develop. Once this occurs the buzzer will make a continuous noise and a quick, firm strike should lead to a hooked fish. Frankly, I prefer the illuminated indicator for night work, for where bream are concerned it gives a far more positive indication than a buzzer.

Handling bream

Although bream have a thick protective coat of heavy slime on their bodies, they are rather a fragile fish and need to be handled with great care. The fins and tail are particularly delicate and tend to split and fray very quickly. The protective slime also wears off very rapidly leaving the small, neat scales exposed. Because of this fragility it is essential to take great care when handling these fish, always making sure that your hands are wet before touching the fish.

Most important of all, make certain never to overcrowd bream in a keep-net, for this probably does more permanent harm to the fish than anything else. When the bream are coming thick and fast, it is very easy to forget about this and cram fish after fish into the net without realising just how much damage is inflicted upon them. Anyone who has seen a really good catch of big bream tipped out of a keep-net will know just what a pitiful sight these fish can be. Gone are the neat, well-made fins and tails; instead the fish will be pathetic, ragged creatures which in all probability are doomed to a slow death from fungoid growths or other diseases. Even the biggest of nets is too small to contain more than five or six good bream at a time, and even then the fish may well be a little cramped. The only real way to deal with this problem is to either carry two or three large keep-nets on all bream fishing expeditions or, better still, to return all the smaller fish as they are caught, and keep only the biggest fish, which will naturally be few and far between. By doing this little harm will come to either the smaller stock fish or the big fish, and this in turn will ensure that there will be plenty of healthy bream left to give sport in future seasons. Every bream angler can help in this form of conservation, simply by purchasing a really big keep-net and using it sensibly.

3

CARP

Less than twenty years ago there were only a handful of carp fishermen in this country, and a 10 lb. carp was regarded as a rare and tricky fish to catch. Little was then known about carp or the techniques required to catch them, and night fishing was seldom practised. Soon after this came the formation of the Carp Catchers' Club, whose carefully selected members dedicated themselves to the problems of catching carp, particularly fish of over 20 lb. in weight. At this time less than a dozen 20 lb. carp had been caught in this country, and the record was held by a 26 lb. fish taken from a lake in the Midlands. Some of England's finest anglers were members of the Carp Catchers' Club, and it was their combined efforts and angling knowledge which finally put carp fishing on the map. The techniques devised by these men have become standard methods among present-day carp fishermen, and have accounted for many of the carp between 20 and 40 lb. which have been caught during the past decade. The carp record is at present held by a founder member of this original group, Mr Richard Walker, whose magnificent 44 lb fish can still be seen swimming round her tank in the London Zoo, a living reminder of the huge carp that exist in various pits and lakes all over England.

The largest carp in our waters are either imported fish, or direct descendants of imported stock, most of which came from the Continent, where fast-growing carp are farmed commercially for eating purposes. Under ideal conditions these Continental king carp have a growth rate of at least 3 lb. per year, which make them ideal stock fish. The variation in scale formation of these fish is too complicated to go into in detail, and most anglers refer to them as mirror, leather, or fully-scaled carp. The latter should not be confused with the old English or wild carp which will be described later in this section. The mirror carp gets its name from the large irregular scales, said to resemble mirrors, which are scattered over its body. There are several distinct variations of mirror carp, some of which are extremely beautiful in appearance. The leather carp is practically devoid of scales and gets its name from its tough leathery skin. These fish are less common than the mirror carp, although by no means rare. The basic body colouring of carp varies considerably from one water to another. Normally the upper section of the body is dark blue, the flanks are chestnut, and the underparts yellow or almost orange. These colours may be pale or exceptionally brilliant depending on the quality of the water in which the fish live, and also the amount of food available to the fish. Rich waters usually produce the most attractive fish. Fully-scaled king carp are, of course, covered with neat attractive scales. The colour of these fish is usually bronze. The true carp is a short, deep fish which has an extremely powerful appearance. Occasionally in overstocked waters which held several generations of carp, the fish began to revert to the wild form, losing their deep-bodied appearance and becoming long and lean in shape. A water which holds mirror or leather carp of this type is most unlikely to produce a really big fish.

TACKLE FOR CARP

Rods

The rod designed by Richard Walker, the holder of the present carp record, is now universally accepted as the best instrument to use for general carp fishing. These rods are marketed under the name MKIV and are constructed from top-quality split cane or hollow fibre-glass. A MKIV is a 10 ft. 2 in. section rod which has a test curve of $1\frac{1}{2}$ lb. This makes it suitable for handling lines of between 7 and 12 lb. b.s. There is a heavier version of this rod on the market which is known as the stepped-up MKIV; as its name implies this is a heavier version of the standard MKIV, and has a test curve of $2\frac{1}{2}$ lb. The S.U. MKIV was designed to catch big carp in very weedy water and will handle lines up to 16 lb. comfortably. The standard MKIV is the most useful rod of the two. There can be little doubt that glass is rapidly becoming the most popular rod-making material, although it lacks the action of good split cane, and has a tendency to be rather light in the tip section. There are plans to overcome this lightness by using carefully designed and placed internal blocks inside the glass blanks. These it is hoped will stiffen the glass up till it corresponds in action and performance with the split cane rods. Glass rods are more robust than cane ones and also keep their shape far longer. This is an important factor for good carp rods cost in the region of £10 to buy, and few anglers are in a position to change rods every two or three years, which is the average life of a well-used cane rod.

Reels

A medium-sized fixed-spool reel is best for general carp fishing, although for close-range work a centre pin can be used quite comfortably. These reels are most suitable for use with light lines, and for float fishing close to the bank a good quality centre pin cannot be bettered. Cheap reels of this type should be avoided. A good centre pin costs between £3 and £6 but if looked after carefully will last a lifetime.

Lines

Although the present record carp was caught on a braided-nylon line, very few carp anglers still use lines of this type, and monofilament lines are now the most popular. Large steps have been taken in recent years to improve the strength of these lines and at the same time to decrease the diameter of the line as much as possible. As a result, there are some first-rate monofilament lines now available, but they are expensive and cost almost as much as braided lines. The best is, of course, always the cheapest in the long run, and line is like most things: you get what you pay for.

Hooks

There is as yet no such thing as a perfect carp hook although there are some good patterns available. Carp are strong, leathery-mouthed fish, consequently a carp hook should have both strength and sharpness. This combination is a difficult thing to achieve, for to be strong, the hook has to be thick in the wire, and a thick-wired hook is difficult to sharpen. The 'goldstrike' hooks are ideal in many ways, being incredibly strong and having a good shape, but they have to be carefully sharpened before use. A carborundum stone should be used to grind down the hook point. The model perfect hook is almost as good as the goldstrike, but is a little too long in the point. Model perfects can be obtained with both long and short shanks. The short shank is easily hidden by the crust and does not project like a long shanked hook. Sizes 2 and 4 are the most useful hooks for all-round carp fishing, but for extra-big baits a size 1-0 can be employed. Always remember that the larger hooks lack the penetration of the smaller patterns, so it is advisable to strike far harder than normal when an extra-big hook is being used.

Landing nets

Even a medium-sized carp is a big fish and a big landing net is an essential item of carp-fishing equipment. Salmon-sized landing-net frames fitted with extra-deep net mesh can be purchased in most good tackle shops. These are suitable for carp fishing, although a little on the small size where really big carp are concerned. A salmon net is, however, quite adequate for carp of up to at least 25 lb. in weight.

Carp and Keep-nets

Several outsize keep-nets are now being marketed as carp nets, but despite the size and depth of these nets they are far from suitable for retaining carp, for carp do not take kindly to nets, and instead of settling down like most fish they will continually try to break through the confining meshes, suffering a great deal of damage in the process. Because of this, keep-nets have been banned on many club and syndicate carp fisheries. There was one well-fished carp pool where the fish were being caught minus tails, fins and even scales, all due to being kept in nets over long periods of time. Some of the carp from this water were in such a pitiful condition that they had to be destroyed. This dreadful state of affairs should be a warning to any carp angler who considers using a keep-net to hold the carp that he catches.

Experienced carp anglers normally carry a large, loosely-woven sack to hold their catch. A fish placed in a submerged sack will come to little harm, for although fresh water can enter the sack, light does not penetrate the sacking and providing a carp is kept in the dark it will make no attempt to escape. Before being used the sack should be thoroughly saturated so that all the air bubbles are forced out of it. When in use the sack should be submerged in a shady place well out of the sunlight. Providing the sack cloth is loosely woven, the fish will suffer no discomfort; a closely-woven sack, however, may kill the fish. Under no circumstances use a sack which has contained chemicals or fertiliser, for this will kill the fish and may even cause semi-pollution of the water. Carp can be kept overnight in a sack and will suffer no ill effects from this enforced confinement. Never keep a fish any longer than is necessary and, wherever possible, weigh or photograph a fish as soon as it is caught and then return it immediately to the water. The night angler, of course, has little choice in the matter and is forced to keep his catch until daylight, and for this purpose a sack is ideal.

Handling Carp

Big king carp are pot-bellied fish, and are easily ruptured. To avoid this happening, all fish should be handled very carefully, and jerky movements should be avoided. When returning a carp, always lower the fish gently into the water and give it time to recover before finally releasing it. Under no circumstances should a fish be dropped or thrown back into the water. Carp have tough, leathery mouths and to avoid tearing the lips too much it is advisable to cut the line and pull the hook through shank first. This is a quicker and far more humane method than the normal technique where the hook point and barb has to be worked out of the lips by force. Artery forceps can be used to unhook carp, and other big fish. These instruments are extremely useful and can be purchased from any good tackle dealer.

Audible bite indicators

For daylight carp fishing, audible bite indicators are unnecessary, but for night fishing a bite indicator of this type is indispensable. There are many patterns available most of which are powered by torch batteries. The most successful are those which work on the antenna principle (see fig. 18). The line is hooked behind the antenna, so that as soon as a fish takes the bait the movement of the line pulls the antenna across, so making electrical contact which automatically makes the buzzer work.

LOCATION OF CARP

Surface-feeding carp are easy to locate, for the loud sucking noises they make quickly pinpoint their whereabouts. Strings of fine bubbles rising from the bottom of a carp water also indicate that the carp are in the swim and browsing along the bottom. Carp also love to bask in the sun and can often be watched in the shallows. Locating carp, then, is usually no problem, but catching them is a far different proposition.

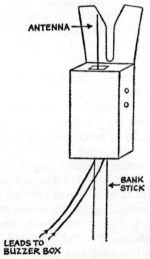

18. Buzzer type indicator.

BAITS FOR CARP

Worm, bread and maggots are the three main carp baits, but these fish will also take potato, banana, green beans, peas, cheese, slugs and fresh-water mussels.

Worms

Large lob or garden worms make excellent carp baits. These can be used either singly or in bunches. Small redworms or brandlings should be bunched so that they form a wriggling ball of food. Carp seem to find these worm balls almost irresistible, possibly because they resemble a large mass of wriggling bloodworms.

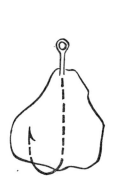

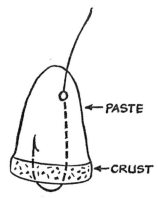

| 19. Flake bait. | 20. Balanced crust/paste bait. |

Bread baits

Bread is one of the most popular carp baits, for it can be used in a variety of ways. A paste made of stale bread and water makes excellent bait. This should be used in large lumps, the size of a golf ball. Flake is another good carp bait. This consists simply of bait-sized portions of the crumb of a new loaf. These should be pinched round the shank of the hook, leaving a fluffy natural section of bread round the point and bend of the hook (see fig. 19). The flake should never be pinched round the point of the hook, for it will go hard in the water and may mask the hook point completely when the strike is made.

Crust

A matchbox-sized crust bait can be deadly. This is a surface bait which should be used close to the bank on weed beds. A mixture of crust and bread paste (see fig. 20) is a useful bait to employ when fishing over a weedy bottom. These balanced baits sink slowly and rest on top of the weed, instead of sinking into the weed as paste will do.

Potato bait

On waters which are inundated with small fish the only bait which the carp angler can use with confidence is a small cooked potato, which although attractive to carp is tough enough to withstand the mouthings of roach or rudd. Small new potatoes make the best baits. These should be boiled, until they just dent when squeezed between the thumb and forefinger. If new potatoes are unobtainable slices of large boiled potatoes can be used. The only practical method of baiting up with a potato is to thread it on to the line with a baiting needle (see fig. 21). Once on the hook, the potato should

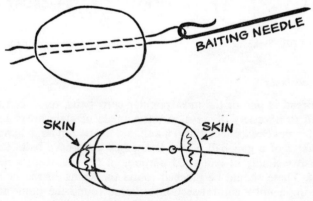

21. Method of baiting up with potato.

be peeled, leaving only a patch of skin at either end to cushion the power of the cast.

Maggot fishing with float tackle

In clear, rich waters, carp often become preoccupied with minute aquatic insects and will totally ignore all the more conventional carp baits, including large worms. Once this occurs the angler must use a natural bait which bears a close resemblance to the larvae and nymphs upon which the carp are feeding. The only easily obtainable bait which falls into this category is the maggot, which bears a close resemblance to a caddis grub. Unfortunately maggots are small baits which require small hooks. Consequently it is necessary to fish with a fine line and light rod when maggot-fishing for carp, and because of this many anglers will not use maggots as bait. This is a mistake, for these grubs are without doubt one of the deadliest of all known carp baits, although they do not conform to the generally accepted theory of big baits for big fish. Avon-type tackle is the best for this form of carp fishing.

Match rods, of course, are unsuitable for handling big fish and should never be used. The Avon-styled trotting rod is ideal, as its easy progressive action makes it suitable for handling light lines, setting hooks and playing big fish. These rods can be used in conjunction with a fixed-spool or centre-pin reel and 4 or 5 lb. b.s. line. This is little more than roach tackle, and a great deal of patience and skill is required to subdue and land big fish on tackle of this calibre. Fortunately many pits have a limited weed growth and a large fish can normally be allowed to take line without fear of its snagging the tackle and breaking free.

Float fishing is the pleasantest and often the most productive method of presenting a maggot bait, for although most carp anglers fish with floatless, leadless tackle, carp seem to show little fear of a float if it is used intelligently. Maggots seem to work best when used in deepish swims close to the bank. particularly when fished a few feet from the side of a ledge (see fig. 22). It is difficult to find an explanation for this, although there is a theory that any insects which are washed over the lip of the ledge from the sun-warmed shallows close to the bank become concentrated on the bottom close to the side of the ledge, and the carp habitually browse along the bottom at these points picking up an easy meal as they go.

Carp are, of course, bottom-feeders and to be most effective the bait should lie right on the pit bed. The laying-on method is ideal for this form of fishing and can usually be relied upon to produce results. Only very light and streamlined floats should be used, and for all-round work a small antennae float is recommended. These floats have great stability and ride steadily in the roughest of water. Stability is as important as visibility where a carp float is concerned, for gravel pits are usually open to the elements and are seldom flat and calm, like well-sheltered lakes. To make the float even more stable and also ultra-sensitive it should be attached by the bottom end only. The float should be set so that at least a foot of line lies on the bottom. Providing one or two of the shot also rest on the bottom, the float will show no tendency to drift.

For maggot fishing, small but strong hooks are essential. Inferior hooks will snap or straighten under pressure. One of the neatest and strongest small hooks is the Sealey short-shanked speed barb hook. A size 12 is suitable for maggot fishing and is quite strong enough for even big carp. Maggots can be used either singly or in bunches, depending upon the ever changing moods of the fish. It is advisable to groundbait a swim with an occasional handful of loose maggots.

Although carp are normally regarded as nocturnal feeders they can be caught at all times of the day, particularly on small

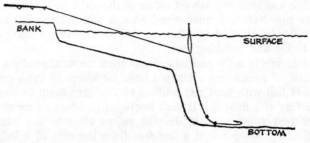

22. Float tackle used close to a ledge.

natural baits like the maggot. Bites are normally registered by the float bobbing two or three times before sliding away across the surface. Hard strikes should be avoided, otherwise the light line may snap under the sudden strain. Great care must be exercised when playing big carp on light tackle and the angler must be prepared at all times to yield line to the fish. Any attempt to force the pace will result in a broken line or rod. No attempt should be made to net the carp until it is thoroughly subdued, otherwise it may make a last desperate, and often successful, attempt to escape.

Legering

Carp are basically bottom-feeding fish and respond well to baits presented on leger tackle. Modern carp anglers now dispense entirely with leger leads, and for casting purposes rely entirely on the weight of the big baits which are generally used for carp fishing. Even light worm baits can be cast quite a long way, and large balls of bread paste or whole potato baits can be cast terrific distances without undue effort.

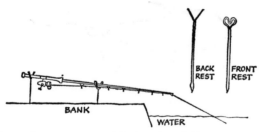

23. Two rod rests are essential when carp fishing. Rod tip should point slightly down at water.

For legering for carp, or any other fresh water fish, two rod rests are essential (see fig. 23). Great care should be taken to ensure that these rests are set so that a taking fish can easily pull line from the reel spool without feeling any resistance to its movements. By setting the front rod rest slightly lower than the back rest, it is possible to ensure that the line can run out freely at any time. Never set the rests so that the rod tip points up instead of down, for a biting fish will have to pull the rod tip down before it can take line, and no self-respecting carp will do that without immediately rejecting the bait. Legering is the simplest of all methods to use. At the same time it is the best method to employ for more carp fall to the leadless leger than to any other known technique.

Stalking carp

One of the most exciting and productive methods of taking big carp during the daytime is to stalk the fish as they lie basking in the sun. This requires a great deal of patience and stealth and accurate casting is essential. Where possible, it is advisable to try only for the fish that bask in the small openings between the weed beds, for the weeds give the angler added cover, and the carp seem to show less caution when surrounded by thick weed. It is, of course, possible to catch fish from open water, but more skill and caution is required to do so, for carp in exposed positions are wary fish, quick to take alarm at any unusual movement or disturbance.

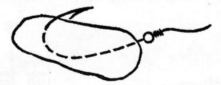

24. Quite a large proportion of hook point and bend should protrude from crust.

The only bait that can be used for this form of carp fishing is breadcrust, for the crust will float even when saturated with water; other baits sink immediately and are useless. Only a small piece of crust should be used, for during the daytime carp seem to prefer small baits. A crust the size of a thumbnail is ideal, and should be used with a size 2 short-shanked hook. Quite a large proportion of the hook point and bend should project from the crust (see fig. 24), for with this form of carp fishing the strike should be made immediately the carp sucks in the bait. If the hook is buried in the crust it may fail to penetrate when the strike is made, and as you only get one chance at a basking carp it is advisable to make sure that the hook point and barb are free from obstruction.

Basking carp are simple enough to locate, for their large size and dark blue backs make them most distinctive even when surrounded by thick weed. Once a fish is spotted it is necessary to get within casting range without disturbing it. This takes practice, but providing the operation is not hurried in any way it is fairly simple to get reasonably close to the unsuspecting fish. Under no circumstances should the crust be cast directly at the fish, for the resulting splash will thoroughly frighten it. Instead the bait should be cast to fall several yards beyond the fish and then slowly drawn back until it is floating close to its snout. Very often the fish will gulp it down within seconds of its arrival, but occasionally the fish will ignore it completely. If this occurs the crust should be twitched slightly. This unusual and unnatural movement will sometimes infuriate the carp to such a degree that it will take the crust in a most decisive manner. Obviously it is possible to watch every movement the fish makes, and as soon as its mouth closes over the bait, a firm fast strike should be made. Any delay may give the fish time to eject the bait and make off. Providing the fish does not sense the presence of the angler it will usually take the bait with confidence. The hotter the day, the more chance of sport, for carp seem to lose their caution on really warm days. This is an exciting but difficult form of fishing which on occasions can be extremely frustrating, for there are days when the fish will vanish at the first movement of a rod.

Suspended crust method

This is a highly effective but little used technique which will often catch carp when all the more conventional methods fail to produce results. Suspended crust tackle is set up in the same way as a standard running leger, the weight being just sufficient to anchor the crust bait, which being buoyant will rise up as far as the trail between lead and hook will allow (see fig. 25). This method works best in fairly shallow water and the tackle should be arranged so that the crust is suspended at mid-water level. This simply means that in a swim that is

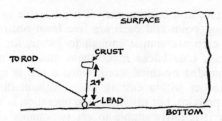

25. The suspended crust technique.

4 ft. deep the lead should be stopped 2 ft. from the hook leaving a trail 24 in. long. Although a crust fished in this way looks unnatural, carp seem to find it most attractive and on hard fished pits where the carp are known to be extremely line-shy the suspended crust method is most useful, for the fish do not seem to notice the line beneath the crust and will often take the bait firmly without any preliminary mouthings. This method works well both during the day and also at night.

On several occasions when using this method in daytime I have been fortunate enough to watch carp approach and ultimately take the bait, and on each occasion the fish has swum round and over the bait, apparently making sure that there was no line attached before taking it. Not once have I seen a carp swim under the bait, and it does not seem to occur to the fish that the line may lead up from the pit bed instead of down from the surface in the normal fashion. This may account for the deadliness of this technique. The suspended crust method is useful for long range work for the weight of the lead and the crust make distance casting simple. Unfortunately, since the tackle is rather bulky it makes a heavy splash as it enters the water, and after casting, the swim must be allowed to settle down before fish can be expected to bite. This may take an hour or more, for, once disturbed, carp are unlikely to feed until they feel the danger has passed.

The suspended worm method

This is a technique used to catch carp which are feeding beneath floating lily pads. Unlike the suspended crust method, no lead should be used, the weight of the worm being sufficient for casting purposes. This is essentially a daylight technique and one that can produce excellent results if used correctly. There can be no question of actually casting the worm to a specific fish. Instead the bait should be cast out so that it hangs suspended over a lily pad, in a likely spot; once in position the bait should be left severely alone to wriggle and twist just beneath the surface. Any attempt to move it may result in the hook point catching in the lily leaves. Carp respond well to worms fished in this manner and probably regard them as completely natural objects, for carp suck a great deal of natural food from the underside of the lily leaves, and are unlikely to pass a worm by without attempting to take it, particularly as the line is hidden by the lily leaves. When using this method it is advisable to watch the area round the bait, rather than watch a bite indicator, for carp will often advertise their presence in the swim by moving the weeds round the bait. By watching for these movements it is often possible to time the strike extremely accurately. In thick weed this is essential, for any delay will give the fish time to run the line round the lily roots, and once this happens a break is inevitable. For all forms of fishing among thick weed, a heavy line is essential, for it is impossible to play a fish in the conventional manner, and any carp hooked have to be held hard and rolled out of the weed as quickly as possible.

Under no circumstance should a hooked fish be allowed to get its head down, for providing you can keep its head up it will flap its way across the top of the weed. Once it goes down, however, it will quickly plunge into the thickest weed it can find. A big fish which does this is almost impossible to shift. If a carp does go to ground and appears to be immovable, there is only one chance of landing it. This is to slack off the line and hope that the fish will extricate itself from the weed and move off. Surprisingly enough this trick often does work, and is always worth trying. Once the fish is on the move maximum pressure should be applied immediately so that the carp is forced to surface. This may sound very unsporting but is better than losing the fish, and leaving it to swim off with the hook still firmly embedded in its mouth.

Margin fishing

Big carp are creatures of habit, and unless disturbed will frequent certain areas regularly. They are particularly fond of patrolling the marginal shallows in search of food and because of this the technique known as margin fishing was evolved. This is a most exciting and often deadly form of angling which requires great patience on the part of the angler. Floating bread crust is the most widely-used margin-fishing bait, for oddments of bread often collect close to the bank and the carp quickly learn that they can pick up an easy living by regularly visiting the bankside swims in search of food. Swims with a screen of reeds lend themselves best to margin fishing, for the reeds hide the angler from the view of the fish and, equally as important, break up the straight unnatural outline of the rod.

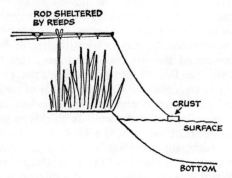

26. Margin fishing with crust.

Once the tackle is set up and the crust lowered on to the surface (see fig. 26), great care must be taken to make no further movement, for carp are ultra-sensitive fish and the slightest movement on the part of the angler will create enough vibration to frighten thoroughly any carp which are in the swim. The line between rod tip and bait should be kept fairly taut, for carp are quick to notice loose coils of floating line and will leave a bait strictly alone if they sense all is not well; at the same time, a slight amount of slack should be left otherwise any wind or slight breeze may cause the rod tip to sway about, which in turn will cause the crust to move and ripple the water. A bait that does this will catch no fish. Warm, still nights are best for margin fishing, for when the water temperatures are high and the surface unruffled, carp are more prone to surface-feed than at any other time. Margin fishing, like all forms of carp fishing, is a waiting game, and many hours may pass before a carp enters the chosen swim. Very occasionally the first intimation that a fish is in the swim comes when the bait is suddenly sucked down without prior warning. More often than not however, the fish will give itself away by making loud sucking noises or by creating ripples as it browses slowly into the swim. Once this occurs the angler must be prepared for action, for providing the fish is unaware of any danger, it will suck down the bait within moments of entering the swim. Sometimes a cautious fish will be encountered which may spend a considerable amount of time trying to overcome its fear and take the bait. Fish like this have usually been caught before and have learned to associate a bait with danger. Carp are quick to spit out a suspect bait, and when margin fishing where the fish can only move a few inches with the bait in its mouth before feeling the drag of the rod tip, the angler must be ready to strike as soon as the bait is taken.

Although swims screened by rushes or other plants lend themselves most easily to margin fishing tactics, open swims can also be fished in this fashion. To do this the tackle should be set up well back from the water, and the line run over a spare rest driven into the edge of the bank (see fig. 27). This rest is essential, for a line laid directly over the grass may catch up when a taking fish runs out the slack line. If this

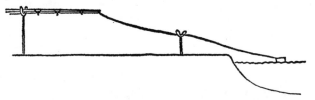

27. A: This rod rest used to hold line above grass, when margin fishing from an exposed bank.

occurs the fish is almost certain to spit out the bait before the strike can be made. Gravel pits lend themselves well to margin fishing, for they often have deep water close to the bank.

Although most carp fishermen use floating bread-crust baits for margin fishing, worms, paste or potato baits can also be used. These should be fished right on the bottom, close to the bank, and are best used during cool, windy weather when the water temperatures are low.

Winter carp fishing

Carp fishing normally finishes during late September, or early October, and few fishermen bother to try and catch carp again until the following June, the belief being that the carp go into hibernation with the onset of winter and do not emerge again until late March or early April, when the water temperatures begin to rise. To some extent this is true, but there are times even in the depths of winter when the fish temporarily come out of hibernation. This normally occurs during periods of sunny weather, when the sunlight penetrates the water for prolonged periods.

After the end of January, carp often become completely active, and the last six weeks of the season can be most productive. As yet few anglers realise this, and winter carp fishing is still in its infancy, although there are signs that ever-increasing numbers of carp fishermen are taking advantage of this extension to the normally short carp season. At best, carp fishing under ideal conditions is a slow pastime, and as might be expected winter carp fishing is no exception to this rule. Obviously it is not possible to go carp fishing at any time during the winter months and expect to catch fish, but by fishing on the brightest days it is sometimes possible to secure a good fish, although even on apparently ideal days many blank trips may be recorded before a carp is caught. I remember one bright winter day when I took three fine king carp in the space of two hours, and then did not take another fish for the remainder of the winter months. I quote this catch to show just how chancy winter carp fishing can be.

From mid February onwards, the situation improves immensely for, unless the winter has been unusually severe, carp will shake off their winter lethargy during early February and for the remaining six weeks of the season often feed well. This short end-of-season period offers the best prospects, and in recent years several carp approaching 20 lb. in weight have been caught during late February and early March. Strangely enough, night fishing often produces fish during this period, for although the nights are extremely cold the carp become active at twilight and feed on into the dark for several hours. All-night sessions are not to be recommended during the winter months, for although the fish may feed for a hour or two, the temperature begins to fall rapidly as the night progresses, and the fish usually relapse into a semi-torpid state until the following day. Although weed-life usually dies down during the winter, it seldom disappears completely and the winter carp-angler will be well advised to fish in the vicinity of these weeds, for carp seem to like to be near weed when they first emerge completely from hibernation.

4

CRUCIAN CARP

The crucian carp is probably the most neglected fish on the British list. Its inbred shyness and secretive habits make it a difficult fish to catch in any quantity, and because of this, and its small average size in comparison to the more popular mirror and common carp, few anglers ever seriously fish for crucian carp, and those that are caught and recorded usually fall to baits intended for roach or rudd. Crucian carp have rather a limited distribution, although they are probably more common than most anglers realise. Many pits contain these fish, and in most cases these waters have been deliberately stocked by private individuals or by angling clubs. Very occasionally, crucian carp make their own way into a water via feeder streams. This is most likely to occur if the stream drains a park lake or similar water which houses a stock of crucian carp, for in time of flood many of these fish are washed into outlet streams, and although many perish in the flood waters, a few will survive and in time find their way into any pit which is fed by the stream in question. This is a rare occurrence, but I know of several pits in both Kent and Sussex which have become stocked with crucian carp in this manner, and one pit which literally became a top-notch crucian carp fishery over night, simply because a nearby lake burst its banks and emptied thousands of specimen crucian into a pit which was situated lower down the valley.

Many clubs are now carrying out extensive restocking programmes, and crucian carp are one of the species being used to repopulate club-owned gravel pits. Crucian carp are attractive chubby fish, with neat scales, bronze sides, and long convex dorsal fins. Although comparatively small, they have a powerful look, and fight extremely well when hooked. Crucian carp vary considerably in size from one water to another, and because of this it is difficult to say what weight a crucian has to attain before it can be regarded as a specimen. Obviously in waters which hold thousands upon thousands of crucian weighing 8 to 12 oz. a 16 oz. fish is a specimen. In other waters where the average weight of fish is higher, a crucian of 2 lb. or more is a specimen. 2 lb. is generally regarded as a good weight where crucian are concerned, and anything over 3 lb. is regarded as an exceptional catch. The crucian carp record is held by a fish weighing 4 lb. 11 oz. Few other crucian carp over 4 lb. have been caught.

There has been, and probably always will be, a considerable amount of confusion between large crucian carp and small common carp, and many an undersized common carp has been set up in the belief that it is a record crucian. To the casual observer both fish look very similar, and as many anglers seldom see either common or crucian carp, mistakes can easily occur. A careful examination of the fish will soon help to identify it. The two main differences are the shape of the back fin, and the presence or absence of barbules on the mouth of the fish. Common carp have long, concave back fins, whereas those of the crucian carp are convex, and common carp have pronounced barbules which are absent on the true crucian carp. The body of the crucian carp is also chubbier than that of the common carp, but the main external differences are the ones mentioned. Careful examination and identification is essential, for a 4 lb. common carp is nothing, whereas a 4 lb. crucian carp is a fish of a lifetime, a truly magnificent catch, a fish that few anglers can ever expect to see.

Crucian carp, like the other carp, are basically a summer species which sink into a torpid or semi-torpid state during the colder months. Occasionally a big crucian carp or two are caught by winter anglers, usually on bright sunny days when the water temperature has risen a few degrees. Few anglers, however, seriously fish for crucian carp after the end of September, and those that are caught are taken by accident on bait intended for other fish.

LOCATION OF CRUCIAN CARP

Unlike the other types of carp, the crucian is a shoal fish, and when one is caught there are usually others in the swim at the same time. Obviously the size of the shoal depends largely on the individual size of the fish it contains, and the largest shoals normally consist of small and medium-sized specimens. The big fish live and feed in small groups which may contain less than a dozen individuals; because of this it is very rare to catch really big bags of specimen crucian carp, and most of the heavy crucian catches reported are made up of fish weighing on average 16 to 20 oz.

Crucian, like most fish, wander about to some extent and are quick to vacate a swim if frightened, but most shoals have selected feeding areas in which they spend most of their time. Crucian carp love weed, particularly of the surface type, for this gives them cover, shade and also provides them with a great deal of natural food in the shape of insects, small water snails and water snail eggs, which they suck from the underside of the floating leaves. This habit often gives the fish away, for the movement of the weed, and the loud sucking noises the fish made, are a sure indication that crucian carp are in a swim. Crucian carp also like to leap out of the water and this helps to pinpoint the whereabouts of a shoal. Failing this, noted swims are well worth fishing, for although they may be well fished throughout the season, crucian are loath to desert a swim entirely, and these hand-fished pitches can usually be relied upon to produce fish consistently, particularly to the angler who is prepared to start fishing at twilight or at dawn.

The best crucian carp swims are normally situated beside dense weed beds, and when visiting a water for the first time, any angler will be well advised to seek out a swim which contains either surface or bottom weed and fish it hard. In waters which contain little or no weed, location of fish can be far more difficult and is in many cases a matter of trial and error. Deepish water close to the bank may yield results, or shallow water well away from the more popular sections of the pit should be fished. Always make sure that you are well screened from the water when fishing these shallows, for crucians are cautious feeders at the best of times, and any unusual shadow or movement is more than enough to panic a normally placid shoal. Crucian carp feed well when the water temperature is high. At these times the shallow swims normally fish best.

When the water temperature is low, due to inclement weather or high wind, the fish move to the deeper water in search of food, and the wise angler should move his pitch accordingly.

TACKLE FOR CRUCIAN CARP

Although crucian carp are game and sporting fish, they can easily be subdued on light tackle, consequently a standard roach-fishing outfit can be used with confidence for most aspects of crucian carp fishing (see Roach chapter). For fishing in heavily weeded swims a slightly more substantial set of tackle can be useful, a MKIV Avon is the recommended rod for this sort of work. This should be used in conjunction with a line of 5 or 6 lb. b.s. so that a fish hooked in the densest part of the swim can be forced out of the weed without fear of smashing the tackle in the process.

Hook sizes

Crucian carp have smallish mouths, and show a marked preference for small baits, and so there is no need to use a hook larger than size eight. The size of hook used depends greatly on the type of bait employed; as a rough guide, the following recommendations give a fair indication of the most suitable hook sizes for the various baits which attract crucian carp. For maggot fishing size 14 or 16 hooks are best, for worms or small bread baits size 10 or 12, and for larger bread baits, big worms or combination baits a size 8 hook should be used. Short-shanked eyed hooks are preferable to the standard shanked hooks normally used by bottom fishermen.

Keep-nets

Crucian carp do not take kindly to small keep-nets, and may severely damage themselves in their efforts to escape from the confines of a small net. In a large net they settle down easily, and any angler contemplating a serious crucian carp campaign will be well advised to buy a big net.

BAITS FOR CRUCIAN CARP

Crucian carp can be caught on all the standard roach baits,

including worms. Maggots are the most popular, for they are both natural and easy to obtain in quantity. These grubs can be used singly or in bunches depending upon the varying moods of the fish concerned. Sometimes these little carp will refuse all baits other than a single maggot on a tiny hook, then the next day will feed wildly on a big bunch of maggots and ignore a single maggot completely.

Bread crust, paste, or flake from a new loaf are the baits most likely to tempt the biggest crucian carp, and when the fish are on the feed, a ragged piece of flake pinched on to the shank of the hook can be deadly. This can be made even more attractive by threading several maggots on to the bend of the hook. These combination baits are little used as yet in this country, but are extremely effective under most conditions, and can often be relied upon to produce bites where all the more conventional baits fail to arouse the interest of the fish.

Brandlings and small lively redworms are also extremely good crucian carp baits, although rarely used by most anglers, probably because they are more difficult to come by than maggots and more messy to use. Worm baits, even when scoured for a few days in moss, are rather soft, and unless the strike is made at the first definite indication of a bite, the carp will probably tear the worm off the hook. Stewed wheat can be a useful bait for crucian carp although it is advisable to pre-bait the swim with loose wheat grains for two or three days prior to actually fishing it, so that the carp learn to feed on the wheat naturally.

Groundbait

Crucian carp respond well to groundbait, and where possible a swim should be thoroughly pre-baited well in advance. Any light sausage rusk or bran-based groundbait is suitable and can be made even more attractive by the addition of maggots and whole or chopped worms. Unfortunately these will also attract small eels, so in waters which hold eels in any quantity it is wise to refrain from pre-baiting with worms or maggots. A few handfuls of groundbait introduced during the time spent actually fishing can also attract and hold the attention of the fish, and it pays to always carry a limited supply of groundbait when after crucian carp.

METHODS OF CATCHING CRUCIAN CARP

Float fishing

Crucian carp are shy biting fish, noted for the delicate way in which they take a bait. Because of this most crucian carp anglers use only the lightest of float tackle, and even then many bites pass unnoticed; more than one angler has started to bring his tackle in and found himself firmly hooked into a big fish which has managed to take the bait without making the float even tremble in the process. Crucians are regarded generally as bottom feeders, but will also feed well off the

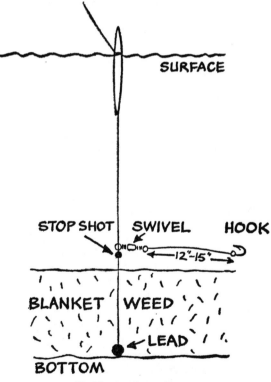

28. Float paternoster.

surface, particularly when the water temperatures are high. Because of this it is sometimes advisable to fish with a self-cocking float (see Rudd chapter) so that the bait sinks slowly and naturally. With this sort of terminal tackle, bites are often easier to detect, for the fish usually take the bait more decisively and then run off with it, so that the float slides off across the surface gradually submerging as it goes. This is a technique which often catches crucian of specimen size. Only a tiny quill float should be used for this kind of fishing. Patches of open water among thick beds of surface weed are ideal places in which to use this method. Maggots or worms make the most suitable baits, for they are both light and natural in appearance, and providing the swim remains undisturbed the fish should take these baits with confidence.

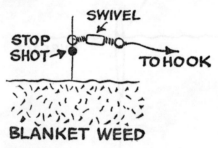

29. Float paternoster detail.

For fishing over thick blanket weed a tiny sliding float paternoster can be a most useful terminal rig (see fig. 28); to make this function correctly the depth of the swim should be accurately determined and the tackle set up accordingly. The line between float and lead must not sag, otherwise many bites will go unnoticed. The length of trail between the hook and the tiny swivel through which the reel line runs should be approximately 12 to 15 in., just enough to allow the bait to settle gently on top of the weed. The stop shot should be attached an inch or two above the calculated depth of the blanket weed so that in operation the weed strands do not foul the swivel or cover the bait (see fig. 29). This is a highly sensitive set-up which requires great concentration, for although bites are normally clearly registered, an instantaneous strike is essential, for as soon as a taking fish feels the weight of the weed covering lead it will eject the bait. Practice is required to overcome this problem, but once the technique has been mastered few bites will be missed.

Legering

Under certain conditions, legering can be an extremely effective way of catching crucian carp, and for night fishing or long-range work it is the only practical method to employ. A conventional leger employing a free-running lead weight can only be used in swims which are comparatively weed free, for in weedy swims the weight of the lead will pull the bait into the weed and hide it from the fish. Even in weed-free swims, the smallest leads should be used preferably on a

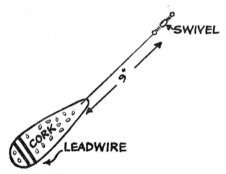

30. Cork leger weight.

sliding link so that a taking fish can move away freely without feeling any check to its movements. In swims which are thick with blanket weed, a wooden or, better still, a cork leger weight should be used (see fig. 30). These useful weights are not produced commercially but can be easily made up at home from long sections of medicine-bottle cork. One cork should yield enough material to make four of these weights.

First, split the cork into four sections, then smooth each section off roughly and rub it down with fine glasspaper. Next, wind a length of fine lead wire round the longest end of the cork, so that it sinks very slowly when dropped into a bowl of water. This is the most important part of the operation for if too much or too little wire is added, the finished weight will fail to function correctly. Having balanced the weight in this fashion, the next step is to thread a 9 in. length of 10 lb. b.c. nylon through the narrow end of the cork with a darning needle and knot it securely with a blood knot (see fig. 31). Finally, add a tiny barrel swivel to the loose end of the nylon, and the cork weight is finished complete with nylon link. A coat of matt green paint can then be added if required. This is a good

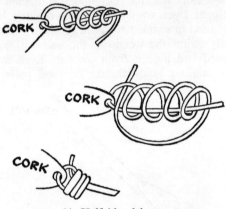

31. Half blood knot.

idea for it helps to camouflage the weight. Small details like this can make all the difference between success and failure and should not be overlooked. Once completed, the weight should be used in the same fashion as a normal link leger; only a tiny dust shot should be used as a stop, for a larger shot will cause the weight to sink far too rapidly. A small section of valve rubber or elastic band can be used in place of a dust shot. This is lighter but may occasionally become wedged in the swivel eye, which will ruin the free-sliding effect of the tackle.

In use, these slow-sinking leger weights are most effective, for even if the weight itself settles in the soft weed the short nylon link is stiff enough to hold the hook length well above the weed (see fig. 32). Bread or combination baits are best, for being light these baits will come to rest on top of the weed. The line between rod top and weight should be kept as taut as possible when legering. It is advisable, however, to tighten the line as gently as possible, otherwise the bait and tackle will be dragged into the weed. A normal bobbin-type indicator should be used to detect bites, and a firm strike should be made at the first definite indication, for bread baits are soft and the fish will have little difficulty in sucking them off the hook.

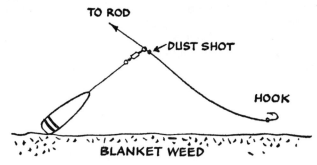

TO ROD

DUST SHOT

HOOK

BLANKET WEED

32. The slow sinking cork leger in use.

Legering is a technique which is as yet little used by crucian carp fishermen, despite the fact that these small carp respond well to leger tackle. With more and more anglers turning to night fishing, the leger is rapidly gaining in popularity, especially as a method for taking the larger than average specimens.

Night fishing

Traditionally, late evening and dawn are the most productive times to go crucian carp fishing. To some extent this is true, but crucian carp also feed well throughout the night, and the angler who begins to fish in the late evening or at dawn is only taking advantage of the beginning and end of the carp's feeding period. More and more anglers are realising this, and night time is now recognised by specimen hunters as one of the best times to fish for large crucians.

The effect of artificial light on crucian carp

True carp dislike artificial light and will often stop feeding at the slightest torch flash. Crucians do not seem to share this fear, and many anglers use a strong torch to illuminate their swim at night. The only advantage to be gained from this is that a float can be used instead of a leger. At no time should the full beam of the lamp be pointed directly into the water. Instead, the light should be aimed across the swim so that the main glare does not penetrate beneath the surface. When a torch is used in this way to illuminate a shallow swim, crucian carp can often be seen crossing and re-crossing the illuminated area. A torch should only be used when it does not interfere with other anglers, for many fishermen dislike the use of light at night and may object strongly if a torch is employed to illuminate a swim.

Surface fishing

Although crucian carp are normally bottom-feeding fish, they will rise to the surface to suck food from the leaves of floating water plants, because of this they can be caught on tiny pieces of floating breadcrust fished among the lily or bistort pads. This can be a pleasant and productive method to use and one which may yield an outsized specimen or two. Any fish hooked on a floating bait fished among thick weed will have to be held hard, otherwise it will quickly snag the tackle and escape, because of this the line should have a b.s. of 5 or 6 lb., far heavier than the line used for normal crucian carp fishing.

5

EELS

The eel is a mysterious creature which spends the bulk of its life in fresh water, but is born and dies in the sea. All the small eels which reach our shores and ascend our rivers start life in the weedy depths of the Sargasso Sea, and after reaching maturity most of them begin the return journey to breed. There is much doubt as to whether or not British eels do in fact complete this return trip, for marine biologists now believe that the two- or three-year journey involved is too long, and that the migrating eels die off *en route*. Not all eels make this final migration, for some female eels never feel the spawning urge, and remain in fresh water throughout their lives. It is these barren eels that interest the specialist eel angler, for they grow to a prodigious size and continue to put on weight until they die. Male eels are of little interest for they have a far lower average size than the female of the species and seldom grow to a weight of more than 2 lb.

Eels are great travellers and during the early part of the year enormous numbers of young eels (or elvers, to give them their correct name) make their way into rivers and streams to begin their lives in our inland waters. Nothing seems to stop these little eels from reaching their objectives, and they are said even to take to the land in an attempt to reach waters which are cut off from inlet or outlet streams. There has been, and probably always will be, much speculation on this particular theory, for there seem to be few people who have ever witnessed eels actually travelling overland, and yet the fact must be faced that eels do inhabit waters which are totally cut off from normal watercourses. A recent theory is that the tiny eels travel via underground streams and enter the waters by way of springs, or through crevices in water-bearing rock. This could easily be the answer, but at present no one can say definitely how eels do arrive in certain waters which have no visible inlets.

The eel record has been held for many years by a fish weighing $8\frac{1}{2}$ lb., but far larger eels are known to exist and with the ever-increasing interest in big eel fishing it can only be a matter of time before eels in excess of the present record are taken. Obviously a barren female eel is something of a freak and because of this really big eels are by no means common, although there are probably more of them about than most anglers realise. Their general shyness and nocturnal habits are another problem that has to be faced by the eel angler, but in time these problems will be sorted out and big eel catches will become more common. No one really knows just what weight a big eel can attain, but there is strong evidence to show that eels weighing up to at least 15 lb. exist in British waters, and it may be that even larger eels lurk in some pools. Big eels are probably hooked fairly frequently by anglers using worm or fish baits, but owing to their vast strength these fish usually break free long before they can be brought to the surface, and as these breakages are usually put down to carp or pike, few anglers bother to fish seriously for eels with extra-strong tackle in the waters where these breakages occur. Small eels, of course, are often prolific, particularly in waters situated within a few miles of the sea. These immature specimens can make a complete nuisance of themselves, for they will attack almost any natural bait, usually managing to completely swallow the hook in the process. Because of this many anglers have a hatred of all eels; this is a pity, for big eels are wonderful fighting fish, and have none of the unpleasant habits of their smaller brethren.

Fortunately eels are rapidly gaining recognition as fine sporting fish which will test the skill and knowledge of any angler to the utmost. To some extent this interest in eel fishing has been largely encouraged by members of the National Anguilia Club whose findings and catches have been reported and recorded in the Angling Press. This is an exclusive club whose members are devoted to both catching and furthering our knowledge of eel angling.

LOCATION OF EELS

Big eels turn up in the most unexpected places; tiny duck-ponds, disused fire tanks, even the Serpentine in London's Hyde Park have produced eels of over 5 lb. in weight, and because of this almost any water is worth trying when eels are the quarry. Man-made pits are extremely good venues, for eels seem to thrive in still water, and the deep clean water of a pit, particularly a pit which has been disused for a number of years, can produce really large eels. Very often gravel pits are fed by streams which give eels easy access to the water, or, like many of the landlocked pits in the Thames Valley, they are situated within a few hundred feet or yards of an eel-producing river or canal. These landlocked pits are one of the best places to seek eels of record-breaking size, for very often the eels which succeed in reaching these waters as elvers are unable ever to leave them again and this enforced captivity deprives them of the opportunity to make the spawning migration; consequently they remain behind growing larger and larger as the years pass. Because of this, pit anglers have the opportunity to fish for big eels under ideal circumstances, and there is every chance that when the existing eel record is finally broken it will be a pit eel which breaks it.

Few average anglers as yet realise the eel-producing potential of wet pits, and at present the waters are at best being fished by a small handful of knowledgeable eel anglers. In time this will change, for as more anglers take to big eel hunting more eels will be caught and reported and more anglers will be encouraged to try their luck with these fighters. In many pits which contain only stunted coarse fish, eel fishing gives the angler the best opportunity of catching a fish of specimen size, and this alone should be enough to encourage anglers to persevere with eel hunting, for a 3 to 5 lb. eel will provide more sport and excitement than a netful of tiny roach, perch or rudd. Luckily, eels can thrive and put on weight in a water in which all the other types of fish have to struggle to find enough food to keep them alive, for the eel is an active hunter, and small fish form a major part of its food chain. Small eels have a nasty habit of tying the line into a slime-covered 'bird's nest', and because of this the average angler regards the eel as a filthy, snake-like creature. This is a pity, for a fine, big eel is a beautiful fish which, although rather slimy to handle, will seldom turn the terminal tackle into a disgusting mess like a small eel, and for sheer fighting ability will match any other fish the coarse angler is likely to encounter.

Eels are, of course, a summer species, which go into semi-hibernation during the colder months. Because of this the eel-fishing season is rather a limited one, unless one is fortunate enough to live in a river board area which recognises no close season on eels.

TACKLE FOR EELS

Normal coarse fishing tackle is hopeless for big eel fishing, and any angler who has the misfortune to hook an eel of specimen size on a light roach outfit will be broken up in the first few months of the battle. By the same token it is silly to use old, well-worn rods, reels and heavy lines when after eels, for these fish soon show up any defects in the tackle. The would-be angler will be well advised to choose his tackle carefully, bearing in mind the waters he intends to fish and the fighting strength of the eels he intends to catch. It is amazing how much strength a big eel possesses and even substantial pike tackle can be badly strained by a bigger than average eel.

Rods

A heavy-duty pike or carp rod of the stepped-up MKIV type is the ideal instrument for big eel fishing for it has both the length (10 ft.) and the strength to subdue successfully a large eel, even in snaggy water. Naturally a rod of this kind is expensive, but it is advisable to purchase top-quality tackle for eel fishing. These rods are obtainable in both split cane and hollow glass; for lightness and durability the glass is best. Good cane is difficult to obtain and even the best split cane tends to take a bad set if used consistently for big fish.

Reels

A salmon or sea-sized fixed spool is the most popular reel with modern big eel anglers. Smaller reels can be used, but their limited heavy-line capacity is a drawback. One or two well-known eel specialists use large diameter centre-pin reels for eel fishing, but these have several disadvantages when compared with a big fixed-spool reel. Long casting is practically out of the question with the centre pin, and, worse still, no matter how free-running a centre pin may be, it will not feed line to a running fish as smoothly as a fixed-spool reel. This may cause a cautious eel to drop the bait.

Line

15 lb. b.s. is the minimum strength of line to use where eels are concerned, and even this may be a little light for use in weedy water, so it is advisable to carry a spare reel spool filled with 18 or even 20 lb. b.s. line. Nylon or braided lines are both good, but the smoothness of nylon makes casting easier.

Hooks

There was a time when any cheap hook was referred to as an eel hook, but these times have changed, and eel anglers now realise the vital importance of using the best and most reliable hooks obtainable, for no matter how good the remainder of the tackle might be the hook is still the direct link between man and eel, and badly tempered hooks can only lead to lost fish. Stainless steel Model Perfect sea-hooks are probably the best hooks available at the present time, for they are both robust and well designed, and exceptionally strong for their size. Sizes 2, 4, and 6 are the most useful, but if big dead-bait is used a size 1-0 hook can be employed.

Traces

Eels have powerful jaws filled with fine but sharp little teeth, which can easily sever strong nylon. A wire trace is therefore essential for big eel fishing. Braided wire is better than single-strand wire, which has a tendency to kink in use and snap under pressure. Nylon-covered braided wire is extremely good, particularly the German products which are usually stained a weed-green colour. Polyester fibre can also be used instead of wire, and has the advantage of being soft and supple. Strong though this fibre is, there is a danger of its parting during a prolonged battle, for the teeth of an eel have a chafing effect on this type of material.

Further thoughts on tackle

All the tackle described may appear ridiculously heavy to the novice eel angler, for even pike and carp fishermen seldom employ tackle as substantial as this; but a big eel is not a fish to be taken lightly, as many an angler has learnt to his cost. A 4 lb. eel is a good fish, and a 5-pounder a specimen by today's standards, so why use tackle that could be used for many forms of sea fishing? The answer is simple. A 5 lb. eel will fight as hard as a 10 lb. pike or carp, and there is always the chance that an eel of record size will find and take the bait. If this happens, it is essential to have the tackle to match the strength of the eel, and to apply as much brute force as possible, for it is impossible to attempt to play a big eel in the conventional manner, and the main objective will be to get the eel on to the bank as quickly as possible. Heavy tackle must of course be used, for light tackle just won't stand the strain.

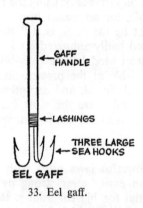

33. Eel gaff.

Gaff or net

A deep, fine-meshed landing net is undoubtedly the most effective instrument to use for landing eels. The mesh, however, must be very small, for given the slightest opportunity even a big eel can wriggle through a small aperture. Some eel anglers use a gaff, which consists of three large sea-hooks lashed to a suitable handle (see fig. 33). This is a most effective weapon, but one that must be used deftly. Any fumbling or mistakes can lead to lost fish and broken lines; once the gaff is in the eel, it is advisable to walk quickly back from the water's edge, for a gaffed eel has a habit of contorting its body up and round the gaff handle and levering the gaff-hook from its flesh. This may only be a reflex action on the part of the eel, but if it manages to tear free of the gaff-hook, and drops to the ground, the sudden weight and shock may cause the line to break. If this occurs well away from the water, the eel can easily be recaught, but if the fish drops at the water's edge it will be off in a flash. Big eels can also be dragged gently up the bank. To do this the eel should be thoroughly played out, then the rod top should be pointed straight at it, and the angler should walk slowly backwards so the eel slides straight ashore. Only well-hooked eels can be safely landed in this fashion.

CHOOSING A SUITABLE SWIM

Almost any section of a pit is capable of producing eels, although most anglers prefer to fish the deepest holes. It does not always pay to overcast when eel hunting, for unless the pit bed is covered in waterlogged tree stumps, sunken machinery or other substantial obstructions which provide the resident eels with adequate cover, most of the fish will live close to the bank in holes or among sunken tree roots. Big eels seem to have distinct territories which are usually within easy reach of their retreats, for, although they may be hooked in clear water, they immediately make a determined effort to swim under some nearby obstruction. Shallow water should never be ignored where eels are concerned, for big eels often venture into the shallows in search of small fry and fresh-water mussels. The shallows are best fished at night. There are times, particularly when a stiff wind has ruffled the water's surface and stirred up the mud and silt in the shallows, when eels of all sizes move into water only a few inches in depth, obviously attracted by the muddied water and disturbed aquatic life. At these times, worms make the best baits, for the eels become preoccupied with small natural baits to such an extent that they will ignore deadbaits completely.

Basically the eel is a nocturnal creature, and night fishing is essential if eels are to be caught consistently. Obviously not everyone wishes to stay up all night, and fortunately one of the optimum times to find eels feeding is from twilight to approximately two hours after dark. Eels dislike cold water, and as the night goes on, temperatures often drop steadily, making the eels disinclined to feed properly. Water temperature plays a most important part in eel fishing, and the higher the temperature, the better the chance of sport. Thunder is said to make eels feed wildly, but it is more likely that the hot, sultry weather which is associated with thunderstorms is the prime reason for this activity. Daylight eel fishing is at best a chancy occupation, for eels usually remain in the holes during full daylight, and even if they do emerge to feed, they keep well away from the bank. It is, however, possible to catch the odd good eel during daylight, particularly in the heat of the afternoon. A freshly-caught deadbait is the best bait for daytime eel fishing. This should be cast as far out towards the centre of the pit as possible. This daylight eel fishing is a slow business, but it is a good way of passing a hot day, and will occasionally yield an eel of specimen size.

BAITS FOR EELS

Eels are predatory fish, which eat almost any small live or dead creature which come their way. The list of baits which can be successfully used for eel fishing is a lengthy one, and includes frogs, small dead unfledged birds, offal, liver, entrails, small mussels, as well as the more normal worms, maggots and fish baits. Blood is said to be a great eel attractor, and some experienced specimen hunters used a hypodermic syringe to pump dead baits full of ox blood before attempting to use them. The eel is also a cannibal and will eat whole small eels, or portions of cut up eel. Obviously not every angler wishes to use frogs, dead birds and entrails, and frankly there is no necessity to do so, for worms and fish baits are equally as effective as the more outlandish baits mentioned, and have the added advantages of being easily obtainable and comparatively clean to use. Bacon fat is a bait which is as yet little used but is extremely good. Large lobworms or garden worms are best used whole or even in big bunches, and these probably account for more big eels per season than any other bait. Fresh dead fish are another fine bait; any small fish will do but shiny fish, such as roach, dace or bleak, are better than dull-coloured baits like perch or gudgeon. The ideal size for a deadbait is 4 to 6 in., although larger fish can be used when fishing waters known to contain very big eels.

Few eel anglers use livebaits, which is strange, for a large eel is an active hunter and will readily accept a livebait. Once again, silver-scaled fish are best, for their natural sheen helps to attract a foraging eel. Slim, narrow-bodied fish make the best live- or deadbaits because their narrowness allows the eel to take and swallow them quickly. With a deep-bodied bait the eel may be forced to bite lumps out of it to reduce it to a suitable size for swallowing. Maggots make quite good eel baits. Unfortunately most other species of coarse fish find them equally palatable, and for this reason few anglers bother to use them regularly for eel fishing.

How to use deadbaits

The simplest and most successful method of mounting a deadbait is to thread it directly on to the trace with a baiting needle. As the diagram shows, the trace is passed through the vent of the bait and out of its mouth. The hook is then tied on and pulled back so that the bend and point of the hook project from the mouth of the bait (see fig. 34). Eels, like all predators, swallow a bait head first; mounting the bait so that the hook is in the head end ensures that when the strike is made the hook should be well inside the eel's mouth. A useful variation of this baiting technique is to bring the trace

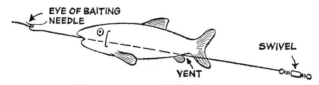

34. How to thread trace through deadbait.

out behind the bait's gill cover, so that the hook bend and
point lies snugly along the deadbait's side (see fig. 35). This
technique has a distinct advantage over the former method,
namely that when the strike is made, the soft side of the bait
tears and does not mask the hook point, a problem that sometimes occurs when the hook projects from the bait's mouth,
for the hardness of the deadbait's head may seriously mar
the penetration power of the hook. Both methods are basically
reliable. A stop shot can be clipped on to the trace close to
the vent of the bait. This serves a dual purpose. Firstly, it
stops the bait from sliding back up the line, and more impor-

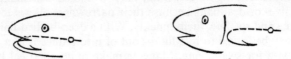

35. Hook point should protrude from jaw of deadbait, or from
behind gill cover.

tant still, it stops a hooked eel from blowing the bait away from
its jaws. This is important, for if the bait stays in place it
serves to gag the eel, which in turn makes it difficult for the
eel to breathe and fight properly—not very sporting, but eel
hunting is a rough game with no rules, and no holds barred.
Fresh baits are essential, for, contrary to popular belief, eels
are clean feeders. Remember, however, to make sure that the
bait's air bladder is broken before casting out, otherwise the
deadbait will float up from the bottom instead of settling right
on to the pit bed in a natural manner. The simplest way of
breaking this air bladder is to crush the bait underfoot; this
not only breaks the bladder but also damages the bait exter-
nally so that in the water its body juices wash out to create a
lane of smell which helps to attract hungry eels.

Methods of catching eels

A plain running leger is the best terminal tackle to use for
deadbait fishing, the length of trace being immaterial. Extra
weight in the form of a swivelled lead can be added if necessary, but weight should be dispensed with or kept to the absolute minimum, for big eels are wary fish and will drop a bait

if they feel the added drag of a large lead. Under normal circumstances the weight of the deadbait is adequate for casting purposes. Deadbaits can also be fished on float tackle. This is useful on pits which have a definite water movement, for by setting the tackle so that the bait just 'trips' the bottom and using a float which is large enough to catch the wind (see fig. 36) the bait can be worked over a wide area. Obviously when night fishing, it is practically impossible to see a float, so the

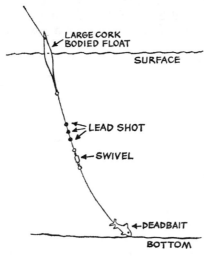

36. Drifting a deadbait on float tackle.

tackle should be set up with a bite indicator of the type used for legering. For this form of eel fishing, smaller than normal baits should be used, for eels will take and swallow a little bait very quickly. This is important for they will 'pouch' the bait before they become alarmed by the buoyancy of the float. When a large deadbait is used the eel will have to manoeuvre it into a suitable position for swallowing and in so doing will almost certainly become aware of the float and drop the bait.

Livebaits

Eels occasionally take livebaits intended for pike and perch, and yet, strangely enough, few anglers ever deliberately fish with livebaits when after eels. There is however an ever increasing interest in this branch of eel fishing, and a number of specimen hunters are carrying out detailed research on the problems and possibilities of livebait-fishing for big eels. A leger is still the most popular technique being used. This varies only slightly from the leger described in the deadbait section, except that a lead of some sort must be used, for a livebait on a free line will quickly entangle the line in some obstruction. A livebait tethered by a weight will simply swim about in a confined area, the extent of this area of movement being determined by the length of trace that is used. A sickly, wounded-looking bait is best, for eels, although active hunters, prefer to

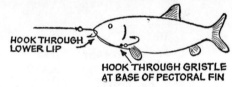

HOOK THROUGH LOWER LIP

HOOK THROUGH GRISTLE AT BASE OF PECTORAL FIN

37. Two hook tackle for use with livebait.

catch their food as easily as possible and because of this may ignore a bait which is too lively. Livebaits can either be hooked through both lips or mounted on a special two-hook tackle (see fig. 37). This is the best method to use, for an eel can easily tear a lip-hooked bait off the hook, something it cannot do when the bait is attached by two hooks. Livebaits can also be fished on float tackle, with the float set so that the bait is suspended close to the pit bed.

Eels and artificial baits

No one spins for eels, and yet a hungry eel can be attracted by the flash and vibration of an artificial lure, and estuary anglers often take eels on baited spoon tackle intended for flounders. To some extent this salt-water method can be adapted for use in fresh water. It works best in waters which hold large numbers of eels, and should be used only in the late evening. The standard baited spoon has the hook attached by an inch or two of nylon. For use in fresh water, this trace

should be 12 to 15 in. in length (see fig. 38). The hook should
be baited either with worm, or a strip cut from the belly of a
freshly-caught roach or similar shiny fish. A standard metal-
flounder spoon makes the best artificial lure, and the tackle
should be worked very slowly so that the spoon bounces across
the pit bed. The flash and glitter of the spoon attracts the
attention of the eels which come to investigate the movement

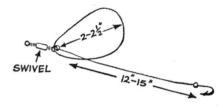

38. Type of spoon rig used to take eels.

and see the bait. A slowly-worked spoon will disturb the mud
and silt of the pit bed, and this also attracts the attention of
any eels which are hunting for food in the vicinity of the
disturbance.

When to strike

Big eels take a bait in a similar way to pike, consequently
the strike should be delayed until the eel has had ample time to
turn and swallow the bait. Premature strikes lead to lost fish.

Removing the hook

Eels are often hooked well down, and this can make the
removal of the hook a tricky operation. Because of this, eel
anglers often prefer to cut the line close to the eel's mouth and
sacrifice the hook. If, of course, the fish is to be kept for eating
purposes, then the hook can be removed at home, but many
modern eel anglers prefer to return their catches alive to the
water, complete with hook. The eel is a tough creature and
will soon get rid of the hook and short length of line, and will
probably resume feeding within the space of a few days.

6

PERCH

The dividing line between small or medium sized perch and big perch is a very distinct one, for once these fish attain a weight of 2 lb. or over they seem to change their feeding habits and haunts considerably. Small perch, for instance, are extremely easy to catch and, on many waters, make a complete and utter nuisance of themselves by gorging down baits intended for other fish. Large perch, on the other hand, become extremely difficult to locate, and even more difficult to catch. In consequence there are very few anglers in this country that can claim to have fairly taken perch of over 4 lb. in weight, and even fish in the 3 lb. to 4 lb. range are far from common despite the fact that many keen and dedicated anglers spend a great deal of time at the waterside in search of these fascinating and elusive giants.

I must admit that I find perch extremely interesting, and whenever the opportunity occurs to fish a water which is known to contain perch of specimen size, I arrive at the venue at the earliest possible hour and don't pack up my rods until well after dusk. Even so, my score of large perch is far from impressive considering the number of hours I have spent in their pursuit. However, I can usually catch a few specimens during the course of an average season, and although I have yet to land a perch of over 4 lb. I feel it is only a matter of time now before I achieve this ambition, for on at least three separate occasions I have hooked, seen and ultimately lost perch which at a conservative estimate would have easily topped the 4 lb. mark. This business of hooking and losing big perch is a problem which I am sure confronts every dedicated perch angler, for the mouth and lips of the perch are of a very delicate construction, and very often the hook will only penetrate the thin membrane that joins the lips to the face of the fish. This membrane will tear very easily under pressure and,

78

once this occurs, the chances are that the hook will simply drop out before the fish can be brought within striking range of the landing net. The only way to counteract this problem is to play the fish on as tight a line as possible.

Unfortunately, it is often very difficult to do this for a hooked perch usually fights with an erratic dart and dash movement, which makes it well nigh impossible to keep a tight line all the time unless, of course, you decide to forget all about playing the fish in the conventional manner and simply hustle it into the net. This is undoubtedly unsporting, but it is the technique which I have now adopted, for, after all, the whole object of going fishing is to catch fish, so I can see little point in being fair and losing a considerable quantity of big fish when, by playing rough, I stand a better chance of landing the majority of the big perch which I hook.

THE RISE AND DECLINE OF A PERCH FISHERY

For some rather inexplicable reason perch waters run in distinct cycles. For a comparatively short period of time they will fish extremely well, producing large perch consistently. After this they go right 'off' and gradually both the numbers and the quality of the fish landed decrease until finally the big fish appear to become extinct leaving behind only the usual hordes of minute perch fry which commit suicide in the traditional manner of the small perch by swallowing each and every worm or maggot baited hook that comes their way. The classic example of this is, of course, Arlsey Lake in Bedfordshire. This large gravel pit probably yielded more big perch in its productive years than almost any other water in the country, with the exception of Oulton Broad in Suffolk which is still producing very big perch year after year. At Arlsey the 'peak' period lasted only a few seasons. During this time, however, many huge perch were successfully landed while other equally large specimens broke free among the tangle of waste machinery which clutters up the bed of this deep pit.

Richard Walker probably pioneered the perch fishing at Arlsey Lake and the long-range legering technique which he developed and adapted for use against Arlsey perch has now become almost standard technique among dedicated perch anglers. Walker himself successfully landed a large number of big perch with this method which, although undoubtedly effective when used against Arlsey perch, has proved to be comparatively unproductive on other waters of a similar type. True enough, it will produce fish on occasions, but at the same time I and several other keen perch anglers have found that variations on this basic technique are required to take perch in other pits and these variations I will discuss at length later in this chapter.

The optimum period for perch at Arlsey Lake lasted for only a limited period. It began in the early 1950s and by 1956 the big perch of Arlsey were almost non-existent. My good friend Frank Gutfield of the Hertfordshire specimen hunters group was probably the last angler to catch a perch of over 3 lb. in weight from Arlsey Lake and, even then, this fish was only captured after Frank had spent incalculable hours at the water-side. There used to be another pit at Feltham in Middlesex which yielded a number of 4 lb. plus perch at approximately the same period as Arlsey reached its peak. Unfortunately, the Council took this water over and turned it into a refuse tip, thereby partially filling it in and at the same time destroying its possibilities as a top-notch big perch fishery. It is extremely difficult to ascertain just why waters of this type suddenly produce quantities of specimen perch, or for that matter why they just as suddenly become unproductive again. Possibly these monsters are from the original stock, or from the first successful spawning of the original fish. This is the most likely suggestion I can offer for, from my own observations on the growth and development of perch in gravel pits, I am convinced that to grow to a respectable size the fish require plenty of food and plenty of space to move about in. The first perch that are introduced to a water get these ideal conditions and for a few years their growth rate is extremely good. Even when they have spawned successfully on a number of occasions they still continue to grow rapidly and probably feed to a great extent on their own offspring. Later, of course, when these original fish have reached the end of their life-span the pit is thick with tiny perch which become more and more stunted by the passage of time. Finally the big fish die off completely, leaving only the hordes of little perch which, by this time, are incapable of growing to a respectable size but are still capable of breeding with a monotonous regularity. This is my own theory on the problem, and whether or not it applies to all big perch pits I cannot say, but on the majority of the waters I fish this seems to be the general trend. It may or may not apply to Arlsey Lake, but here again I cannot say for, strangely enough, I have never actually fished for big perch at Arlsey. In consequence my knowledge of this particular fishery is limited to various articles I have read on the water and the discussions I have had with experienced Arlsey perch fishermen.

It is interesting to note that, as the numbers of big perch in a water decrease, so other species come to the fore. In one water I know the fish that came in were carp, while on another water roach became the predominant species. There is little doubt in my mind that there are far more large perch about than most anglers generally realise. This is particularly true of gravel pits, for often these man-made lakes are so large and so deep that it is difficult to fish more than a fraction of the pit without the aid of a boat, and as most pit owners refuse to allow boats on the water because of the dangers involved, there seems to be little solution to this problem.

In my experience disused pits are most likely to produce specimen perch than pits that are still being worked, and it seems that perch grow faster in clear water than they do in water which is clouded by particles of suspended sand and silt. Pits that are still in production are invariably 'cloudy' and I have yet to take a perch of over 2 lb. in weight from this type of water. It may be that perch hunt more by sight than anything else. The large size of the fish's eyes in comparison to its body suggests this to be more than a theory, and when using small livebaits for perch fishing the shiny baits, such as bleak, roach or dace, usually produce more runs per session than gudgeon or small perch which are of a darker colour.

TIME OF YEAR

The bulk of the big perch which came from Arlsey Lake were caught during the back end of the season, and from my own angling diary I find that the majority of the specimen perch which either I or my companions have landed have also been winter-caught fish, quite a number having been taken during January and February. I feel, however, that I haven't spent enough time summer fishing for perch as yet to draw any complete conclusions on this subject, and it may well be that a warm weather perch programme would produce first-class results, for I remember on one occasion while fishing for carp with legered lobworm bait I took five perch over 2 lb. in weight in less than twenty minutes' fishing. The only drawback to perch fishing in warm weather as I see it is the problem of locating the fish in the first instance, for when the water temperatures are high, the perch will tend to wander about it all over the pit. This, of course, doesn't occur nearly as much during prolonged periods of cold weather for then the perch congregate in the deeper holes and gullies where, providing you are able to drop your baited tackle into one of these spots, the chances are it will land within reach of the fish. Naturally enough, when the fish are grouped in certain areas you stand a far greater chance of success, but even so I am still convinced that it pays to fish hard during the summer months as well.

It seems to me that during the colder months perch feed rather spasmodically. Bright days, however, usually produce more runs than dull days, and when the sky is cloudy or overcast, the fish often feed for an hour or two in the middle of the day when the light is at its brightest. This again adds weight to the theory that perch hunt more by sight than by smell.

GROWTH RATE OF BIG PERCH

To the best of my knowledge, very little is known about the growth rate and development of big perch, although scale readings were taken from several of the large Arlsey fish. One specimen weighing 4 lb. 2 oz. was eight years old, while another fish an ounce or two under 4 lb. in weight was approximately seven years old. In all possibility the growth rate of the Arsley fish was exceptionally high, and I doubt very much whether fish from other waters would show such rapid development.

GENERAL TACKLE

Although the ardent perch angler is quite likely to encounter

fish weighing between 3 lb. and possibly 5 lb. at some stage
of his career, the chances of the fish putting up a prolonged or
even vigorous battle are very slight, for by nature the perch
is not a particularly dashing fighter, despite the fact that many
angling writers in the past have portrayed the perch as a
gallant and very strong creature. It is only necessary to look
closely at the tail of the fish, which in comparison with its
thick hump backed body is relatively tiny, to see that although
the perch has all the spirit in the world it is physically incapable of putting up much more than a slight resistance when
hooked, and even a big perch on the lightest of roach tackle
can be handled quite easily providing, of course, the fish
doesn't manage to sidle under or round some underwater obstruction. At Arlsey, several very big perch were lost in this
way, but then it must be remembered that these fish were
hooked very close to various items of submerged machinery
and in consequence had to be literally pulled through these obstructions before they could be pumped back towards the shore.

Bearing in mind, then, that the perch is incapable of fighting
to any great extent, it should be possible to catch these handsome fish on ultra light tackle. Unfortunately extraordinarily
long casts are often required to drop the bait on to the known
feeding grounds, and as this calls for the use of a lead weighing three quarters of an ounce or more, a reasonably substantial line and rod has to be used. At one time the rods I employed were MKIV Avon's used in conjunction with fixed-
spool reels and 6 lb. b.s. line. It didn't take long, however, to
realise that these beautiful rods had their limitations. For a
start the strain of 'punch' casting a heavy lead a considerable
distance soon began to weaken the cane and, more important
still, I found that I missed more than a reasonable percentage
of bites. This undoubtedly occurred because the light-actioned
rods were almost incapable of driving the hook firmly home at
the extreme ranges I was casting. Once I realised these faults,
I quickly changed to a pair of standard MKIV carp rods. The
reels, naturally enough, remained the same, but I stepped up
the line strength another pound to counter-balance the extra
strength of the rods. Although this tackle may appear in theory
to be far too heavy for perch fishing, in practice it works
extremely well. The Avon type rods are of course quite suitable

for closer work, and being of a lighter construction they do add more interest to the fishing, but for all-round use I thoroughly recommend a pair of true carp rods.

Hooks

At various times I have tried a wide variety of hooks for perch fishing. Trebles I have long since discarded for, although they have great hooking power, they can damage a fish very badly. This I dislike intensely for, whenever possible, I like to return the fish I catch alive and unharmed to the water. Double salmon fly hooks, on the other hand, I have used with great success, particularly when using a livebait on leger tackle (see fig. 39). Apart from this, I have always found a size two or four round bend hook to be perfectly satisfactory.

39. Double salmon fly hook for use with livebait.

Setting up the Rods

Big perch, like carp, are extremely cautious fish, and at the slightest check to their movements they will eject a suspect bait and depart in panic to a safer area. For this reason great care should be taken when setting up the rods. Two rod rests for each rod are a must and any projecting grass or weed should be cleared from between the rests, otherwise the bite indicator may catch up as a taking fish pulls line from the reel spool. It is quite a good idea to pull a small groundsheet down on top of the grass (see fig. 40) then it will be almost impossible for the moving line to catch up. Each individual angler has his own favourite type of bite indicator. For perch fishing, however, the lightest possible indicator should be employed. A piece of silver paper folded over the line (see fig. 41) is quite good. Remember, however, that a taking perch will usually make a long initial run. Consequently, it is necessary to open the pick-up of the reel and also to make absolutely certain that the line can run freely through the silver paper indicator and not jam up in any way. Silver paper indicators work extremely well providing there is little or no wind. If, however, there is even a moderate wind the paper will tend to blow from side to side and this can be annoying for often the swaying movement will cause a few coils of loose line to slip off the reel spool and, unless you are careful, this may result in a nasty tangle. To overcome this possibility a matchstick can be attached to the rod butt by means of an elastic band (see fig. 42) and then the line can be lightly clipped under the matchstick. This will beat the wind completely, but at the same

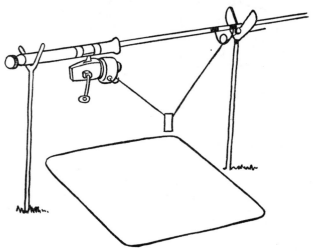

40. Small groundsheet between rod rests.

41. A small fold of silver paper on line makes a good bite indicator.

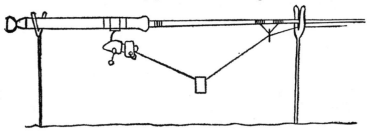

time the slightest pull from a hungry fish will unclip the line
and allow it to run out freely. This is a favourite method of
mine, and one which I use successfully for many species of
coarse fish.

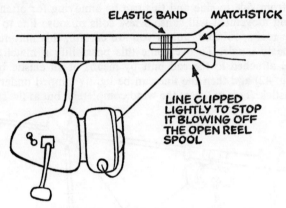

42. Matchstick method of beating wind problem.

Baits for perch fishing

Although large lobworms accounted for the majority of the
big perch which were caught at Arlsey Lake, I am sure that
livebaits would have worked equally well, providing that it
were possible to not only cast such a bait a considerable distance, but also to ensure that the bait arrived on the bottom in
good shape. The casting problem is comparatively easy to
overcome, but unfortunately the pressure of the deep water
would quickly kill a small fish if it were suddenly dropped
rapidly into the depths. In actual fact, the change in pressure
worked in reverse on the perch that were taken, for many of
the fish arrived on the surface with bulging eyes and distended
swim bladders. Luckily many revived sufficiently to swim off
when released, but others died, and this may well have been
another reason why the big perch at Arlsey Lake finally became extinct. To be fair, however, Arlsey is deeper than the
average pit and, although I frequently livebait for perch in
depths of between 20 and 30 ft., the change of pressure does
not seem to affect my baits in the least.

Gudgeon have always been regarded as the best livebaits for perch fishing, but in the light of my own findings I would say they are definitely inferior to 'shiny' fish, i.e. roach, dace and bleak. Much of my perch fishing in recent years has taken place on gravel pits in the Thames Valley area, and as a rule I usually spend the first hour of the day on the river catching livebait. As any Thames angler knows, London's river is inundated with bleak which, although make a nuisance of themselves to the general coarse fisherman, are a boon to the angler that requires enough livebait for a day's pike or perch fishing. Bleak are so easy to catch, in fact, that nowadays I rely upon them for perch fishing, and although legend has it that they are extremely frail, delicate little fish which die very easily when used for bait, I have always found them to be the exact reverse, and on many occasions I have known them to outlast roach and dace baits.

Many perch anglers still use tiny livebaits and discard anything over three or four inches in length as being too big. This is nonsense, particularly if you intend to fish for very big perch. Wherever possible I use baits between 6 and 7 in. long, for I have found in the past that small baits produce on average small fish. There are, of course, exceptions to this rule, but these are few and far between. Consequently I find it better to employ a big bait and wait for the better quality fish to turn up, but even so I still occasionally take perch of 1 lb. or less on my big baits, so it just goes to show how big the mouth of even a small perch can be.

Worms of course have always been first-class perch baits. Unfortunately they too produce a great many smallish perch, but even so it always pays to carry a tin of large lobworms just in case other baits are unobtainable.

Deadbaits

In recent years, deadbaiting for pike has become a recognised technique, and many big fish have fallen to large deadbaits fished on float or leger tackle. Deadbaits will also catch perch. At Wadhurst Lake in Sussex both Gerry Berth-Jones and I took quite a few largish perch on a whole, or half a dead roach or rudd. The first few specimens we landed came by accident, for originally the deadbaits were intended for eels. Once we realised, however, that big perch were about we modified our tackle and, in consequence, our deadbaits accoun‑ ted for a number of fish weighing between 2 lb. and 2 lb. 10 oz. Not exceptional fish by national standards, but even so very big for the water in question. Later I tried deadbaits for perch on other waters, and on one deep disused gravel pit near Lon‑ don Airport dead fish produced a number of specimens. Dead‑ baiting is, however, a slow method of fishing, and unless you are prepared to spend a considerable length of time waiting for a 'run' to develop, my advice is to stick to the more conven‑ tional techniques. It is extremely interesting to note that all predatory or semi-predatory fish will take deadbaits with confidence.

Artificial baits

Perch, particularly the small and medium sized fish, are greatly attracted by the flash and glitter of an artificial lure, and for the angler interested only in sport and a good bag of fish a day's spinning with ultra light tackle on a reasonable pro‑ ductive perch pit can be great fun. Spinning, however, is seldom practised by the angler interested in catching very big perch, for although the odd outsized fish does succumb to the attractive sparkle of some well finished spoon, or plug bait, artificial baits on average do not seem to appeal to the really large fish. Even so, I occasionally spend a happy day, armed only with a rod, reel and landing net, spinning for perch, and I must admit I enjoy these outings immensely. Also they make a break from the big fish routine which can become a little tedious at times. At one time I had access to an almost raw bit which held a large number of perch up to about 2 lb. in weight. Invariably I used to spin for these particular fish, and quite by accident I discovered a method of catching the bigger fish fairly consistently. This occurred simply because my line developed a tangle shortly after I had cast my long 'wobbling' spoon out. I suppose I had retrieved approximately ten yards of line when I noticed the tangle. Naturally I stopped winding in, and started to unravel the mess. The bait obviously sank down to the bottom where it lay motionless for two or three minutes. Finally I cleared the line and was just about to start cranking the reel handle again when the slack line between the rod tip and the surface of the water suddenly tightened and I found to my amazement that I was hooked firmly into a 2 lb. perch. There was no question about the fact that this fish had picked up a stationary spinner, and I wondered whether or not this was one of those thousand to one chances that occasionally do occur in angling or whether I had hit upon a new technique. The latter applied for I experimented for the remainder of the day and proved conclusively that the perch in this particular pit would pick up a stationary lure, providing I first retrieved it for a few yards before allowing it to sink to the bottom.

Later I tried the idea on two other waters where it also worked well. It seems to me that the perch first see the lure moving along in the conventional manner and they then give chase, following close behind the bait. Suddenly the lure appears to die, and flutters slowly to the bottom and lies still. The following perch then comes to a halt and studies the bait. Finally it is convinced that somehow or other it has contrived to kill the bait, so down it goes, picks up the bait and moves off, apparently disregarding the weight and the hard unnatural feel of the 'fish' in its jaws. This technique seems to work best in shallow waters, and I can only recommend it for use in snag free pits, otherwise your pocket will be unable to keep up with the amount of tackle you will lose. In Holland a similar technique is used to catch huge roach, and roach-bream hybrids and over there the favoured bait is a tiny fly spoon.

Float fishing

Although it is quite possible to catch perch at all times of the year on float tackle, I have always looked upon float fishing for perch as a summer technique, and as a rule I tend to discard it in favour of the leger with the onset of winter, mainly, I suppose, because I feel that during the early part of the season when the water temperatures are consistently high the perch will often swim and feed within easy casting distance of the bank. Later on, when winter is well on its way and the temperatures start to decrease, the perch forsake their summer haunts and retire to the deeper areas well away from the shore. There are, of course, no hard and fast rules on this subject, and I have no doubt that many big fish have been close to the bank under almost arctic conditions. Even so, this is not a general occurrence and I, for one, always try to cut the lucky chance aspect of angling to the minimum.

43. Old fashioned round bodied perch float, a quill is much better.

Floats

There are still many traditions in angling, and one of these is the so-called perch float (see fig. 43). This, like so many traditional bits of tackle, is a badly designed abomination which should have no place in the true perch fisherman's tackle box. For a start, its ungainly shape makes it awkward to cast and, more important still, the shape of the float is designed to create as much resistance as possible to a taking fish. The only thing I can say in its favour is that it is capable of supporting quite a large livebait, but then so will a long pelican or swan quill, and at the same time these streamlined floats offer the minimum resistance to a biting perch. This is extremely important, for large perch are quick to drop a suspect bait, and nothing seems to alarm them more than dragging a big float about.

Float tackle for perch fishing need not be elaborate, and providing the float is capable of supporting the bait satisfactorily, that is all that matters. Normally, I set the float so that the bait is suspended a foot or so off the bottom. Very occasionally, if I happen to notice a perch actively chasing small fry close to the surface I will reel in and adjust the float so that the bait hangs just beneath the surface, but normally I prefer to fish close to the bottom for that is where I expect the perch to be. During the summer months when there are plenty of small fish about it is possible to attract large perch to your baited tackle by throwing out quantities of bread and bran groundbait. This does not interest the perch, but it does attract hordes of small fry, and these in turn bring in the perch. On some waters it is also possible to attract perch by throwing in handfuls of earth to cloud up the water. I only recommend this technique when you are fishing completely alone, for you could easily disturb someone else's swim by indulging in this 'groundbaiting technique'. On pits that are still being worked it often pays to fish in the vicinity of the dredgers or mechanical scoops, for once again the perch are often attracted by the disturbed and muddied water. Under these circumstances worms make the best baits for, after all, when you think about it logically, it is obvious that a great many worms and grubs will be uncovered by the digging operations and many of these will find their way into the water where the perch will be waiting for an easy meal. The fish may even become preoccupied to such an extent with this form of food that they will refuse to even look at a livebait.

Legering

As I said earlier, long range legering tactics have probably accounted for more big perch during the last twenty years than any other method yet devised. For leger fishing with worm bait the length of 'trace' between hook and lead can range from 12 to 24 or even more inches, but if you intend to use a legered livebait I would suggest that the distance between hook and lead should be increased to between 4 and 6 ft. This will make long casting rather difficult, but if you can manage to over-come this problem I think you will find that your catches will increase accordingly. On one gravel pit I fish it is very rare to get a run on short trace tackle, and on several occasions I have used two rods, one made up so that the bait was within 7 ft. of the lead and the other set so that the livebait had $5\frac{1}{2}$ ft. between it and the lead. For every fish I caught on the short trace rig, I took four with the other tackle. Frankly I don't think that it is the lead that puts the perch off; instead I am sure that before the fish will take the livebait it will chase it about for a while. On the long trace the livebait has more scope to dodge about a bit, and this probably excites and in-furiates the hunting perch to such an extent that it takes the bait in a firm and decisive fashion before it has a chance to escape.

On the shorter link tackle the livebait hasn't nearly as much chance to skip about, and in consequence the attacking perch may become suspicious and refuse to take the bait. This theory is in many ways backed up by the antics of the silver paper bite indicator on the short trace rod, which often lifts, trembles and twitches indicating that the livebait is alarmed. Seldom, however, do these movements develop into a full blooded run. Occasionally when I have wound the tackle in after a bout of 'twitches' on the indicator I have found the livebait to be dead, often with large patches of scales missing from its back and sides. I think in these cases small perch were responsible, for on several occasions I have watched three or four perch in the 6 to 8 in. class harrying roach or rudd almost as big as themselves. Obviously perch of this size were unable to swallow the other fish, but their hunting instincts were so strong that they attacked regardless of the large size of their quarry. It is of course possible that I am completely on the wrong track, and that large perch were responsible for the battered state of the bait. I have even tried striking at these 'twitching' bites but as yet I have never succeeded in hooking a perch in the process. Usually when a perch takes a legered livebait the bite will follow a distinct pattern. First the indicator will rise smoothly as far as the first rod ring, then the line will start to stream out at a steady speed. As a rule I wait until the running fish has taken 8 to 10 yards of line, then I engage the pick-up of the reel and strike the instant I feel the movement of the taking fish against the rod tip. When I first started perch fishing I used to strike at the first indication of a run, but I lost so many fish because of this that I learnt to control my reactions and to delay the strike until it was reasonable to suppose that the perch had had sufficient time to turn and swallow the bait. Even so, I still find that I fail to hook quite a high proportion of bites. This is annoying and extremely frustrating, but try as I might I can find no complete solution to the problem.

Drift line fishing

This is a floatless leadless method which can be extremely effective when the perch are feeding close to the bank. The tackle is very simple and the weight of the livebait makes it sufficient for casting purposes. As no float, or other indicator is used for this form of fishing, I find that it pays to always hold the rod. At the same time, the line should be watched with great care, and as soon as it begins to move rapidly away or behave in any other suspicious manner you should be prepared to 'feed' line off the reel spool, so that the taking fish will feel no resistance to its movement. I occasionally use this method in the late summer or early autumn, and, as a rule, I travel light and rove continuously along the banks in search of fish. Perch lend themselves well to this style of angling, and providing you don't clutter yourself up with too much equipment you can have an extremely pleasant and often productive day's fishing.

The behaviour of perch in keep-nets

Legend has it that if you hook and lose, or land and release a perch in your swim, it will in some way contrive to warn the fish in the area of the danger. How they achieve this I have yet to ascertain; presumably by some form of telepathic communication or possibly by a transmission of fear. I can't say that I fully believe that this in actual fact does happen, although on several occasions I have lost or released fish in a productive swim, which has then immediately become to all intents and purposes devoid of fish life. This is quite possibly sheer coincidence, but at the same time it doesn't pay to take chances, and for this reason I usually carry a big keep-net on most of my perch fishing expeditions, the only exception being when I intend to adopt the roving style of fishing. Then it doesn't matter anyway, for I can easily move on once a given area ceases to produce fish. When confined in a keep-net, perch have a habit of playing dead. Whether or not this is a deliberate form of self-defence, or simply an aftermath of the shock which they must have received during the battle, nobody knows, but it is very distressing to see a big and very beautiful perch floating on its side, or even 'belly up' in the net. Try releasing it however and you will find just how quickly an almost dead perch can recover. Believe me, they need no second opportunity for they will usually be away like a flash, so don't worry too much if you find you have a net containing nothing but dead or dying perch. Instead tap the net with your landing net handle and watch the way they come to life.

7

PIKE

Big pike seem to thrive in gravel pits, and a yearly analysis of the big pike catches recorded in the Angling Press would probably show that well over 50% of the specimens reported come from gravel pits in various parts of the country. Whether or not any of these pits are capable of producing a record pike remains to be seen, but there is strong evidence to show that they could, and with more and more anglers taking to pike fishing it can only be a matter of time before a veritable monster is hooked. Specimens up to 33 lb. have been taken during the last season or two, and most years a few fish weighing between 28 lb. and 32 lb. are caught. Many of these fish are returned alive and apparently unharmed to the water where presumably after a suitable recuperation period they begin to put on weight again. Unfortunately little work has been done on the growth-rate of gravel-pit pike, and most of the very big pike are returned by the captors before a scale or two can be removed for growth study. It is therefore difficult to come to any definite conclusions on the age and development of these big fish, which in turn would provide valuable information as to the general growth-rate of pike from the waters that do produce these monsters.

There has always been a great deal of controversy on the size of specimen pike, but I am sure that if an overall average was taken of all the pike caught during the course of a single season, it would probably show that the average pike in this country weighed approximately 5 lb. This may sound ridiculous when compared with the weekly winter reports of pike over 20 lb. in weight, but look at it logically and it is obvious that these fish make news, simply because of their size, and the number reported in comparison with the number of anglers out pike fishing will show that these big pike are very few and far between even on the noted pike waters. Many an expert pike angler has yet to take a specimen above 20 lb. in weight, and yet it is common to hear anglers talking of 20 lb. pike as though fish of this calibre are an everyday occurrence, which they most definitely are not. Any pike over 10 lb. can be classed as a good fish, and any pike over 15 lb. weight as a specimen. It takes just as much skill to catch a 15 lb. pike as a 20-pounder. It is just the law of averages that for every 20 lb. fish there must be a far higher proportion of 15-pounders, and because of this it is more likely that the bait will be taken by a 15-pounder than a 20-pounder. Small pike can be a nuisance and considerably lower the average weight of the pike caught in most waters. To some extent there are ways of overcoming the small pike problem. These will be discussed later in this chapter.

Every fresh water angler will be familiar with the outward appearance of the pike. Its long, lean body, huge head, and cruel teeth give it a wicked look. Because of this many anglers who should know better make a habit of ill-treating any pike they happen to catch. Probably this hard-heartedness and cruelty where pike are concerned is motivated by fear that the fish will bite. This is a pity, for a pike properly handled is no more dangerous than any other fresh water fish and should be treated with the respect it deserves. Far too many fine pike are clubbed to death in this fashion, and then discarded at the end of the day or taken home to be displayed for a day or two before being consigned to the dustbin. This is a dreadful state of affairs, and should be stamped out by clubs and river board authorities. Match anglers, of course, argue that the pike eat all the small fish and generally ruin a fishery. This is far from true, and many of the most productive pits hold large numbers of fine roach, perch, carp, tench, etc., as well as many big pike. It is far more likely that the presence of pike in a pit helps to keep the other fish in check, thereby raising the average size of fish caught. Diseased fish also fall easy prey to hungry pike, and this helps to control any outbreaks of disease in a water. Pike also eat pike and to some extent keep themselves in check by their cannibalism. Occasionally, of course, a pit is found which contains thousands of stunted pike. This situation is rather rare, however; at Staines in Middlesex there are several day-ticket pits, which hold large numbers of pike up to at least 20 lb. These same pits also contain huge shoals of fine crucian carp, which at 2 to $2\frac{1}{2}$ lb. in weight make ideal food for the larger pike. Despite this, the crucian carp continue to thrive and keep up a high average size. Without the pike, however, it is doubtful whether these pits would produce a sizeable crucian, for the fish would multiply at such a rate that they would exhaust the food supply and quickly become stunted. Basically it is simply a balance of nature problem, and the pike play a major part in controlling this balance. Many similar examples could be quoted but this would be rather pointless. Obviously in a small water which only holds a limited stock of fish, or in a pit which is stocked with trout, pike can be an absolute menace, but in a normal well-stocked coarse fishery pike are an asset. Pike also provide the ordinary angler with the opportunity to catch really big fish, without undue expense. For this reason alone the pike is well worth conserving. Many clubs, of course, are well aware of these factors and treat the pike accordingly; this is an intelligent approach which should be adopted by all modern anglers. With time, it undoubtedly will be, but until this state of affairs is reached and anglers in general learn to appreciate or at least to tolerate pike, many hundreds of fine fish will be thoughtlessly destroyed.

FEEDING HABITS OF PIKE

Although predatory by nature, pike will at times eat almost anything that the angler can offer. Normally, however, the pike is a fish-eater and lives mainly by preying on shoal fish of various types. Small pike usually prefer to catch fresh food, but big pike often become scavengers, and are quite ready to pick up and swallow any dead fish they happen to come across. Strangely enough, they do not seem to mind overmuch if they eat almost rotten fish, although I think they are more inclined to go for a fresh dead fish if given the choice. Under normal circumstances pike usually lurk in a suitable place until a shoal of small fish venture close enough to attack, then they lunge out and snap up a victim before the shoal has time to scatter. In gravel pits, however, I am inclined to think pike become rovers and instead of hanging about in one specific area they tend to wander about in search of food. Obviously a man-made pit will seldom provide much in the way of cover for the pike, consequently the fish are forced to hunt far more actively than river or natural-lake pike, which usually have reed beds, tree roots or even fallen trees to provide them with cover.

BAITS FOR PIKE

Live fish make the best all-round pike baits, and as pike are not fussy it does not matter really what type of fish you employ as bait. Roach, rudd, dace and gudgeon are the most used livebaits in this country, mainly because they are easily obtainable in most districts. Small bream also make good pike baits, as do perch. On several occasions I have used very small pike as bait for big pike and found them to be good fish catchers. During the last ten years or so dead-fish baits have become popular with pike specialists, and there can be little doubt that deadbaits are extremely effective. Deadbaits have several advantages over livebaits, particularly if the angler concerned dislikes the idea of impaling a live creature on a large hook and casting it out to almost certain death in the jaws of a hungry pike. Moreover deadbaits can be obtained with the minimum amount of trouble, for large pike show a distinct liking for herrings, which are usually available from a local wet fish shop. Why pike accept a sea fish in this way no one can say, but in all probability they are attracted by the oily flesh of the herring, and being lazy creatures are quite content to pick up an easy meal instead of chasing about after the shoalfish upon which they normally feed. Most herring-caught pike are big fish and although I have occasionally seen a smallish one caught on herring, the usual run of fish is over 10 lb. in weight, much higher on average than pike caught on livebaits. For the specialist angler this is very important, for by fishing long and hard with herring baits the small fish can usually be avoided and when a pike does come along, the chances are it will be of specimen size.

TACKLE FOR PIKE

Big pike rarely put up an impressive battle when hooked, although they will occasionally make long powerful runs in their attempts to escape. Even so, it is essential to use fairly substantial tackle for most forms of pike fishing simply to cast effectively the large baits which are normally employed. A light rod, although delightful to use, will not take the strain of casting heavy live- or deadbaits, nor for that matter will it have the power necessary to set a largish hook firmly into a bony tooth-filled mouth. Tackle shops are full of short fibreglass instruments, labelled as pike rods, most of which are modelled on the type of rod which is popular in America. American anglers, however, fish from boats, and restrict themselves to spinning for their fish and for this style of angling the tiny 6 and 7 ft. rods are entirely suitable. English anglers, of course, seldom get the opportunity to boat fish, and tend to live- or deadbait instead of spin. In consequence, the little single-handed glass spinning rods are practically useless for pike fishing in this country, although far too many anglers still buy these rods, and struggle to use them. A good pike-fishing rod should have a minimum length of 10 ft. There are now many specially designed pike rods on the market, most of which are 10 ft. long and built in two sections. Continental pit fishermen are using rods of twice this length for pike fishing, but as yet these are not available in this country. Good-quality split cane is practically unobtainable these days, and because of this shortage most rods that are designed to cast heavy baits are manufactured in hollow fibre-glass. Several good fibre-glass pike rods are available, the Sportex Hornsea being one of the best. This is a rod designed by a top pike fisherman for catching big pike in Yorkshire's famous pike water Hornsea Mere. As a rod it has much to recommend it, for it is robust enough to cast large deadbait without becoming damaged in the process and yet light enough to be handled with absolute comfort, throughout a long day's fishing. A stepped-up MKIV carp rod can also be used for pike fishing. Rods of this type have a test curve of approximately $2\frac{1}{2}$ lb. and are capable of handling lines of up to 16 lb. b.s.

Spinning rods

The rods already mentioned are too heavy for general spinning, for a far lighter rod is necessary to cast light artificial lures any distance. A standard MKIV carp rod is most suitable for general spinning, short rods should be left severely alone. The MKIV has a test curve of approximately $1\frac{1}{2}$ lb. and is designed for use with lines between 7 and 12 lb. b.s. This rod is quite capable of stopping a really heavy pike, and yet is light enough to give the utmost sport with medium-sized fish.

Reels

Medium- or sea-sized fixed-spool reels (see section on Long-range Fishing) are best, although for bankside work a large diameter centre-pin can be used. Multiplying reels are expensive and require a great deal of practice if they are to be used efficiently.

Lines

Monofilament lines are best, although good quality braided line can be used if preferred. A set of spare reel spools should be carried, each loaded with a different b.s. strain of line, ranging from 10 lb. b.s. up to 16 lb. b.s.

Hooks

Treble hooks are essential for pike fishing, and it is advisable to buy only the best quality hooks, for pike are heavy fish and badly tempered hooks will soon give way under the strain of playing a big fish. Many pike anglers use very big treble hooks. This is a mistake, for a big hook is difficult to set, whereas a smallish hook will usually penetrate fairly easily. This is important, for a pike has a bony mouth.

For livebaiting with medium-sized baits, a size 8 treble hook is quite large enough, but with big baits and deadbaits, size 4 or 6 trebles should be employed. These larger hooks are less likely to tear out of the bait during casting. Very big trebles should have no place in the modern pike angler's tackle box. Single hooks can, of course, be used for pike fishing but are not advisable when big pike are known to be in a pit. Always buy loose treble hooks and make up the terminal tackle at home. Traces made up like this cost less than half the price of made up ones bought from a tackle shop.

Trace wire

Pike have long sharp teeth which can easily chafe through

ordinary nylon. Because of this it is advisable to use a length of wire between reel line and hooks. This wire should be attached to the reel line by means of a swivel. There are several types of wire on the market, the best and most supple being the braided wire. This is obtainable with or without a nylon covering; the nylon-covered wire is less supple and of a larger diameter than the plain braided wire. For this reason the plain wire is preferable. Single-strand steel wire is also obtainable. This has a nasty habit of kinking during casting and then snapping under pressure. This unpleasant fault spoils an otherwise ideal product. Trace wire can be bought in 5 to 25 yard coils. By buying it this way and making up traces at home, a good deal of money can be saved. Never continue to use a trace which has become twisted or kinked, for the wire may have become seriously weakened and will probably break under strain.

Floats

The most popular pike float is still the old-fashioned bulbous 'Fishing Gazette Bung', an outdated monstrosity if ever there was one; these floats seem to have been designed to create as

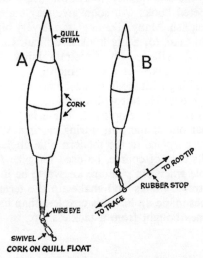

44. Pike floats.

much resistance as possible, and yet pike anglers, who through their own experience should know better, still buy them, despite the fact that there are many light, streamlined sea floats in the shops which make ideal ready-made pike floats. A useful bung can be made from a quill and a couple of medium-sized medicine-bottle corks (see fig. 44a). The corks can be roughly shaped and painted if required and are buoyant enough to support a sizeable bait. A float of this kind should have a wire eye and a swivel lashed to the bottom. The float can then be turned into a 'slider' without dismantling the tackle (see fig. 44b). Good pike floats are long and slim; short fat floats should be avoided.

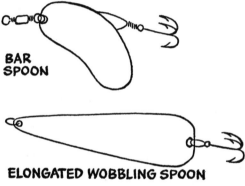

BAR SPOON

ELONGATED WOBBLING SPOON

45. Elongated wobbling spoon.

Artificial baits

Artificial lures are legion, and many are designed simply to catch the angler rather than the fish; it is wise to choose one's lures with great care, making absolutely certain that only the more serviceable patterns are purchased. Bar spoons (see fig. 45a) and large Wobbling spoons (see fig. 45b) are both well designed, and can usually be counted on to catch fish. Fancy lures should be avoided, for they are rather expensive, and spinning can be a costly occupation even when the cheaper lures are employed. Plugs make good pike baits, and will often catch pike when other lures fail. Single- or double-jointed plastic plugs are best (see fig. 46). Choice of colour is a matter

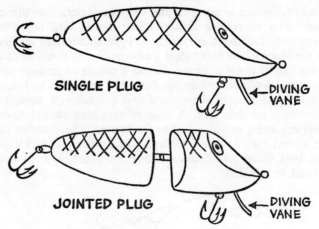

SINGLE PLUG

DIVING VANE

JOINTED PLUG

DIVING VANE

46. A: Single plug. B: Jointed plug.

of personal preference, although I find that the darker patterns are often the best fish catchers. Striped plugs, which look like perch or small pike, are exceptionally good. Light-coloured plugs, on the other hand, seldom seem to arouse the interest of the fish. There are dozens of other baits, some designed to look like swimming frogs, mice, etc. These should be left alone, for they are gimmicks which serve little practical purpose.

METHODS OF CATCHING PIKE

Livebaiting with a float paternoster

For livebaiting in deep-water swims close to the bank, or in heavily-weeded swims where a bait fished on standard float tackle would quickly become snagged up, the float paternoster is the obvious answer, for this tackle is easy to cast and providing it is set up properly in the first place it will anchor the bait firmly in the required spot. Fixed floats are not really suitable for use with paternoster tackle and a streamlined sliding float is essential. A sliding float with a drilled centre tube is preferable to a float with wire side rings (see fig. 47), for these tend to cushion the effect of the strike and occasionally the line will catch up round those rings during casting. Neither of these problems occur with a tubed float.

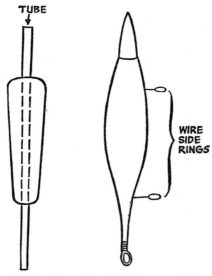

47. Tubed sliding float. Wire side ring type sliding float.

Although the float paternoster (see fig. 48a) looks complicated, it is in fact extremely simple to set up and use. The line
having first been run through the rod rings, a tiny bead or small
shirt button should be slid on to the line. This will eliminate
the possibility of the rubber stop jamming in the top of the
float. Next, the float can be run on to the line, followed by the
wire trace. This trace should be attached to a small barrel
swivel. The reel line should pass through the open eye of this
swivel (see fig. 48b). A three-way swivel could be used, but in
practice this type of swivel is inferior to the barrel swivel, for
it does not give to the movement of the livebait which results
in line twist. The trace should be stopped by a small shot
placed approximately 30 in. up the line. The weight should be
knotted to the end of the reel line and a section of rubber band
tied to the line above the float. The tackle is then ready for
use. The depth of the swim should be carefully ascertained by
repeatedly moving the rubber stop up the line until the float
just cocks nicely on the surface (see fig. 49). If the float lies
flat or sinks, further adjustment is necessary, but once the

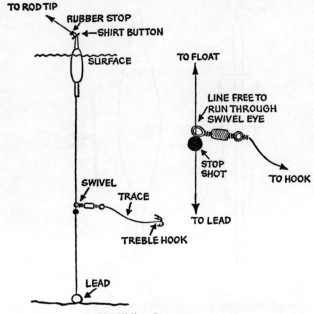

48. Sliding float paternoster.

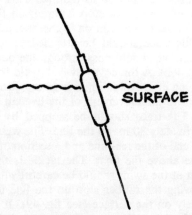

49. Float should just cock on surface.

float cocks, the stop is correctly positioned and the tackle can be baited and put to work. For paternoster fishing the bait should be liphooked on a single treble hook (see fig. 50). Traces carrying two treble hooks are more nuisance than they are worth on paternoster tackle, and have no advantage over the single treble hook. A liphooked bait will last far longer, and remain far livelier than a bait hooked through the back and sides, and, most important of all, will suffer far less than a bait mounted on two hooks.

50. Bait should be liphooked on single prong of treble.

Summer pike fishing

Pike are said to be slow to recover from spawning, and for this reason many angling clubs and river boards stipulate in their rule books that pike fishing must not commence before 1st October. Consequently the majority of anglers regard the pike as a winter fish. There is, of course, very little logic behind this archaic rule, for pike are one of the first fish to spawn, and the so-called big, end-of-season specimens recorded are usually gravid female pike on the verge of shedding their spawn. If the weather is particularly mild after Christmas then in all probability pike will spawn during February or early March at a time when anglers are legally entitled to catch them.

Later, during the summer months, when the fish have fully recovered and are in a fit state to give the best of sport it is illegal in many areas to go pike fishing. Summer pike are often long and lean by comparison to the fat, sleek winter fish, but this does not mean they are out of condition and require protection. Far from it, in fact, for it is really the bloated spawn filled winter fish which should be conserved. In a few areas, of course, pike can be fished for at any period during the coarse-fishing season, and where this rule applies pike can

offer the summer angler fine sport. As a general rule pike
spend the summer months in shallowish water, where, like
most big fish, they like to bask in the warmth of the sun. Most
pits have a shallow area, and this is where the summer pike
angler should concentrate his efforts. It is amazing how really
big pike will live and feed in water barely deep enough to
cover their bodies. Pike hooked in the shallows can be relied
upon to put up a terrific battle when hooked, and will usually
fight far harder and longer than a fish of similar size hooked
in deep water.

Summer pike seldom have to hunt for food, for the shallows
are usually thick with small fry which provide them with
ample sustenance. Because of this prolific food supply summer
pike have a tendency to become preoccupied with small live
fish, and will seldom bother to take a deadbait. During the
warm months livebait is easy to come by and an hour's fishing

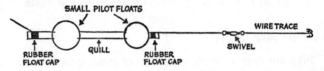

51. Norfolk weightless dumbell float for use in shallow water.

with light tackle will usually yield enough small roach, perch
or gudgeon for a day's pike fishing. Pike, like most big fish,
live in close proximity to weed or reed beds and often give
away their position by lunging at the shoals of small fry in
the vicinity of their retreat. A bait cast out to fall close to the
disturbance will usually be taken within a few minutes. Failing
this the bait should be fished close to the weed beds. In shallow
water a weight on the line can be a disadvantage and it is
advisable to use a weightless float. Norfolk pike experts use
this weightless float technique to fish the shallow Decoy
Broads, and the float they use (see fig. 51) is entirely suitable
for fishing the shallow sections of gravel pits. This float can
be easily made up at home by sliding two medium-sized pilot
floats on to a suitable length of swan or peacock quill. The
pilot floats can of course be purchased from any fishing tackle
shop. Once again the bait can be liphooked on a single treble
hook, although a trace carrying two trebles can be employed

if necessary. If the water in the shallows is, for example, 3 ft. in depth, then the float should be set at 18 in. This will stop the bait from diving to the bottom, but still give it plenty of room to move about and attract the attention of any hungry pike that is lurking in the vicinity. As the tackle is weightless, the float will simply lie flat on the surface, and will offer little resistance either to the bait or to any pike which takes the bait.

Shallow-water pike fishing can be a most exciting occupation, for the fish will often leap right out of the water as it takes the bait, and every movement of a hooked fish can be clearly followed. During the middle part of the day, summer pike are often lethargic creatures, but in the late afternoon or evening, when the air and water temperature starts to drop, the fish often begin to feed madly.

Night fishing

Although pike have been caught after dark, very little research has been done in this field; it will not, however, be long before the possibilities of taking big pike during the night are thoroughly explored by one or another of the noted specimen-hunting groups. Night fishing in the dead of winter does not appeal to many anglers, and it is doubtful whether or not even the hardiest of pike fishermen would care to spend an entire winter's night at the waterside, but most anglers would be happy enough to extend a short winter's day, by staying on for an extra two or three hours after dark. On many gravel pits the pike only begin to feed during the last hour of daylight, and evidence would show that the fish continue to search for food until well after full dark. Because of this it is reasonable to suppose that night fishing could be highly productive where pike are concerned. Only long hours of night fishing can prove this point, but they would probably be hours well spent.

Long-range winter fishing

Pike fishing on really large gravel pits can be extremely frustrating, for the larger pike often lurk in the deepest water well beyond casting-range of the bank. If time is no object, then it is simply a matter of sitting back until one of these big fish ventures in from the deeps and takes a bait presented close in, but this can be a lengthy occupation and there can be no guarantee even then that fish will be caught. One well-known angler, Ron Barrett, spent a total of twenty-four days doing just this, and on the last day took a pike of exactly 20 lb.—a good fish by any standards, but was it really worth the length of time spent to catch it? Approximately 200 hours of solid fishing were required to catch this fish, and one pike in 200 hours can hardly be described as interesting fishing. Even so, the angler's perseverance must be admired, and as any specimen hunter knows, big fish are few and far between at the best of times. By getting the bait right out into really deep water, however, there would have been a far greater chance of making contact with a big pike in a far shorter period of time.

Obviously, depositing a bait into an area of water which is beyond normal casting-distance creates several problems. These obstacles can with a little patience be overcome, although very often at the expense of accuracy. At long range this is to be expected, and it does not really matter anyway, for, providing the bait is dropped into deep water, it is im- material whether it is directly in front of the swim or not. A boat is, of course, the answer, but few angling clubs or gravel pit owners allow the use of a boat, due to the obvious danger involved should an accident occur well away from the bank.

One of the simplest methods of increasing effective casting- range is to buy a wide-spooled, sea-sized fixed-spool reel. I say wide-spooled, for many of these reels are fitted with deep, narrow spools. These will hold plenty of line, but empty rapidly during casting, and this drastically cuts down casting distance. With a wide spool this problem does not occur and distance casting can be easily achieved. Originally these big reels were designed to hold heavy line for beach fishing, but by backing up the spool with old line and then adding 200 yards of 12 or 13 lb. b.s. line to fill the spool correctly, these reels are perfectly adaptable for use in fresh water. Another advantage with these large reels is that the increased overall size of the reel makes for a rapid retrieving rate, and thus it is extremely simple to keep in direct contact with a fast-moving fish hooked in deep water.

Deadbaits are the only natural bait suitable for this long-range deep-water work, and where casting-power alone is to be used to get the bait out, a substantial rod is essential, for a deadbait is heavy and a normal rod simply will not take the strain of casting a 6 or 8 oz. bait 60 to 80 yards. Short rods are useless for this sort of fishing, and a rod with a minimum length of 10 ft. is essential. Most gravel pit pike specialists make up their own rods from hollow glass beach-caster blanks. These are normally obtainable in lengths of 11 to 12 ft. For use with a sea-sized fixed-spool reel, extra-large rod rings should always be used (see fig. 52). Small-diameter rings are useless, and will cut down the casting potential of the rod considerably. An outfit of this type is extremely powerful and to some extent rather unsporting, for even a big pike can be

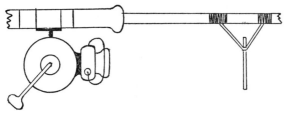

52. Extra large rod rings are essential for use with sea-sized fixed spool reels.

subdued with the minimum amount of fuss. When using these long range tactics great care must be taken when striking, for with a 12 or 13 lb. b.s. line it is easy to break up on the strike. To some extent the elasticity of the line will cushion the strike, but even so it is advisable to be as gentle as possible.

Obviously this heavy tackle does not appeal to everyone and there are of course other methods of getting the bait out without employing big reels and light beach-casting rods, the simplest being to float the bait out by means of a 'balloon boat' (see fig. 53). Although highly effective, this technique is far from accurate and is entirely dependent on the wind. To fish this method properly, it is necessary to choose a swim with the wind at your back, so that the balloon float will sail straight out and away from the bank. Any short length of flat driftwood can be used as a boat, and a round balloon tied to one end of the wood acts as a perfect sail. Round balloons are best, for, having a large surface area, they pick up and hold the wind better than any other shape of balloon. The baited tackle should be laid in the centre of the wood but should not be attached in any way to it. This having been done, the boat and bait should be taken as far out from the bank as possible and allowed to drift off with the breeze. There is no need to use a heavy rod for this type of fishing although a fixed-spool reel is essential, for once the wind catches the balloon sail, the line must run freely from the reel spool; the slightest check will drag the bait off the boat and the whole process will have to be repeated. It is advisable to pay off the reel by hand so that no snag can occur. In this way the bait can be floated out to a distance of 100 or 150 yards without any trouble, although it

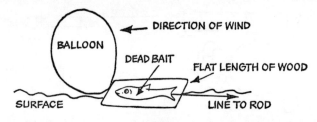

53. Dead bait.

is practically impossible to place a bait accurately when this method is used for the wind is certain to cause the makeshift boat to drift either to the right or left of the swim. In a big pit this is not very important providing that the bait comes to rest in really deep water. Once the boat has reached the required distance, the reel pick-up should be closed, and the line tightened until the bait slides off the 'boat' and sinks. The boat of course will be lost but providing the bait is in position this is of no consequence. Once the bait has reached bottom, the line can be tightened, the rod placed in the rests and the reel pick up flicked into the open position. After this it is simply a matter of patience.

Legered livebait

Livebaiting with float tackle is not always the most practical

method of fishing, and there are occasions when it is advisable
to dispense entirely with a float, and use a plain running leger
to present the bait to the fish. Legering can, of course, be an
extremely boring way of fishing, and many anglers prefer to
float-fish simply because it is more pleasant to sit and con-
template a brightly coloured float than to sit gazing at the line
between rod tip and water. There are occasions, however, when
the use of a float can ruin any chance of sport. This applies
particularly to heavily-fished pits, where most of the pike have
at one time or another been caught, and have learned to drop
a bait which is suspended beneath a large buoyant float. A bait

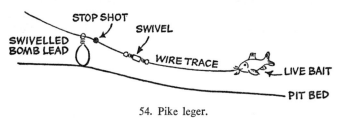

54. Pike leger.

presented on leger tackle will not frighten the fish, and because
of this the leger is by far the most practical, although not the
most pleasant technique to employ under these circumstances.
The leger is also useful for fishing awkward swims where a
float would probably drag the bait into some obstruction, or
away from the most likely pike lie. There is nothing complicated about a pike leger (see fig. 54), which is made up in the
same way as a normal running leger.

There are numerous methods of attaching the livebait. The
two most practical are to lip-hook the bait on one prong of a
treble hook, or to make up a special snap tackle and hook the
bait through the lip and the back (see fig. 55). This is the best
method if long casting is necessary, but a livebait hooked in

55. Special snap tackle for legering.

this way dies rather quickly whereas a lip-hooked bait will remain lively for hours on end. The distance between lead and bait should be approximately 2 ft. but longer or shorter traces can of course be used without adverse effect on sport. With the snap tackle described, an early strike can be made with every confidence, but where one treble hook is used it is wise to give the taking fish ample time to take the bait well into its mouth before attempting to strike and set the hook.

When to strike at a taking pike

Pike usually follow a set pattern when taking a live- or dead-bait, and by carefully interpreting the movement transmitted through the line or by the actions of the float, it is possible to calculate the exact moment when the strike should be made. Generally when a pike picks up a bait it will move off on a first run, the length of this run varying from a few feet to 30 or more yards. After this the fish will stop and turn the bait so that it can be swallowed head first. Once the fish begins to move away for the second time it is safe to assume that the bait is well inside its mouth and the strike should be made accordingly. Any further delay will result in the fish being hooked right inside its throat, and this will probably mean that it will have to be destroyed before the hook or hooks can be retrieved. To make absolutely certain this does not occur, many experienced pike fishermen wait until the pike stops after its initial run, rapidly count up to ten, and strike immediately this number is reached. Occasionally a fish will be lost by this practice but more often than not the hook will engage neatly in the corner of its jaw.

How to strike at a pike

In most forms of angling, a firm upward strike is essential, but in pike fishing, striking in this fashion is a mistake, for the pike's mouth is both bony and tooth-filled and an upward strike will cause the hooks to bounce off these bones and teeth. The only safe hook-hold is the corner of the mouth, which, being gristly, offers firm purchase for a hook; it is necessary, therefore, to strike sideways and in the opposite direction to that in which the fish is moving. If the pike runs off to the right, then the strike should be made to the left. If the fish makes off to the left, then swing the rod round to the right and drive the hook firmly home from that direction. A pike cleanly hooked in the corner of its jaw will seldom escape by biting through the trace, for all the wire will be clear of its teeth. It is also rare for the hook to tear out when lodged in this part of the pike's anatomy.

Methods of landing pike

There was a time when all pike caught were automatically destroyed regardless of size or weight. During this period a gaff was always used to land the fish. Nowadays these instruments are rarely used except by experienced pike fishermen. In untrained hands a gaff can be a lethal weapon, and because of this many forward-thinking angling societies stipulate in their rule books that gaffs must not be employed under any circumstances. This in many ways is a wise ruling, for even an expert can make a mistimed stroke with a gaff and drive the gaff-hook into the body of a good fish. Once this happens the pike concerned has little chance of recovering from the wound. If a gaff must be used, then great care should be taken to ensure that the gaff-hook only penetrates the thin skin, covering the outer angle of the pike's lower jaw (see fig. 56). Even this can be dangerous, for if the gaff-hook sticks through the fish's tongue, then in all probability the pike will bleed to death.

Most modern pike fishermen prefer to dispense entirely with

+ MARKS THE ONLY
SAFE PLACE TO
GAFF A PIKE

56. X marks the only safe place to gaff a pike.

the gaff and use a carp-sized landing net for the larger fish. This is a far more humane method and is to be strongly recommended. Small pike up to 8 or 10 lb. can be easily landed by hand, a firm grip behind the gill covers giving a strong hold. When using this method, great care should be taken not to insert the fingers into the fish's gill slits, for any damage to the delicate gill rakers will result in a speedy death for the fish. Under no circumstances must a pike be picked up by the eye sockets. This is an old fashioned and barbaric practice which fortunately seems to be dying out.

Extracting the hooks

Pike have large teeth and strong jaws which can unintentionally inflict quite a nasty wound to an unwary hand. Because of this a medium-sized pike gag (see fig. 57a) should always be carried. Very large pike gags should have no place in the pike angler's bag, for these are brutal, powerful instruments which can easily dislocate the jaws of even a very big pike. Once the gag is in position, the catch can be slipped and the jaws of the fish prised open, a long disgorger or, better still, surgical forceps (see fig. 57b) can then be used to extract the

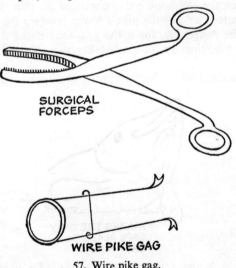

SURGICAL
FORCEPS

WIRE PIKE GAG

57. Wire pike gag.

hook or hooks. In the case of a lightly-hooked fish this operation is simple, but if the hooks are lodged in the back of the
pike's throat the angler is faced with the problem of trying
either to probe for the hooks or to cut the trace as close to the
hooks as possible and release the pike complete with hooks, in
the hope that it will manage to get rid of them and eventually
recover. This is not as unlikely as it sounds, for pike happily
eat perch which have spiky dorsal fins, and a hook is probably
no more unpalatable to a big pike than a set of dorsal fin
spines. If, on the other hand, a determined attempt is made to
remove the deeply-set hooks, there is a good chance that the
fish will become badly damaged in the process and subse-
quently expire. A pike returned with hooks still embedded has
a fifty-fifty chance of survival.

Deadbaiting

Pike are lazy fish, and the larger they grow the less inclined
they become to hunt actively. Instead, they are content to become scavengers, living for the most part on dead fish which
they pick up from the bottom. On hard-fished waters pike are
well supplied with food of this kind, for the mortality rate of
small bait-sized fish which have been handled and confined
in keep-nets is high. Because of this pike become so used to
finding an ample supply of easily obtainable food that they
tend to lose their hunting instincts and show more interest in
deadbaits than in live ones. Although pike anglers have known
this for many many years, it is only during the last decade
that deadbaiting has become a recognised and widely used
technique, due mainly to the research and experiments con-
ducted by the Taylor brothers of Aylesbury, whose writings
on the subject prompted other keen pike anglers to experiment
with deadbaiting methods in waters all over the country. These
experiments have proved so successful that deadbaiting is now
regarded as one of the premier pike fishing techniques.

To some extent deadbait fishing is a selective method, for as
a rule very large baits are used, and because of this and the
fact that big pike are basically scavengers, the average size of
pike which fall to deadbaits is far higher than the average
weight of fish taken by livebaiting or spinning tactics. There

are exceptions, for a pike is capable of swallowing a fish practically as large as itself, but as a rule it is only pike close to or over 10 lb. in weight which take deadbaits. A carefully kept seasonal record of the big pike recorded in the Angling Press will show that well over fifty per cent of the pike over 20 lb. caught in this country fall to deadbaits of one sort or another. Deadbaiting is a comparatively slow method of fishing, and any angler wishing to concentrate on this technique must be prepared to spend many inactive and fishless hours. Perseverance will usually pay off in the long run, and it does not do to become discouraged and change to the more productive methods of livebaiting or spinning, for sooner or later a very big pike will find your deadbait, and a fat 20-pounder is worth a dozen 3 to 5 lb. fish. There are, of course, the red-letter days when the big pike really start to feed and then it is possible to make magnificent catches of fine pike. Days like this are, unfortunately, rare but do occur during most normal seasons.

Few anglers like the idea of impaling a live fish on a hook, and because of this deadbaiting is becoming increasingly popular, for by using dead fish as bait, any angler can fish with a natural bait, without causing pain to a live creature. How much pain and discomfort a livebait feels we do not know, but anyone who has driven the prong of a treble hook into the back or side of a livebait must have noticed that a convulsion passes through the bait as the metal penetrates its flesh. Because of this average-sized livebaits should be lip-hooked. This considerably reduces the cruelty angle of livebaiting. With a deadbait, of course, there are none of these problems, and the bait can be mounted on a series of hooks without worry.

Providing it is large and reasonably fresh, almost any fish will make a good deadbait, irrespective of whether it is a fresh-water or sea-water species. Fresh herrings are the most widely used deadbaits, for they are easily obtainable from wet fish shops, have a large average size, and are covered with bright silver scales which make them resemble roach, rudd or other natural fresh water fish. A dozen herrings are normally more than enough for a day's fishing, but it is wise to carry an ample supply in case the pike are feeding more freely than normal. Although herring are regarded as the best deadbaits, other sea fish can be used as well; mackerel in particular are being used in increasing numbers by deadbait enthusiasts, in the belief that the shape of a mackerel and its marbled markings make it resemble a small dead pike. Big pike being true cannibals are quite prepared to eat their own offspring. Recently a 39 lb. pike was caught on a dead pike which was estimated to weigh 4 to 5 lb.—a fine example of the cannibalistic tendencies of big pike. A week or two before this huge fish was landed, a Norfolk angler successfully boated a 40 lb. pike, which accepted a dead roach bait. These fish, which were two of the largest pike ever caught in this country, both fell to deadbaits, proving that as a big fish technique deadbait fishing has a great deal to recommend it. Sprats can also be used to good effect where pike are concerned. Unfortunately they are small in comparison to herring or mackerel baits, and tend to attract the unwanted attention of the smaller pike.

Groundbaiting for pike

Pike fishermen regard the use of groundbait with mixed feelings where pike are concerned, although there can be little doubt that the judicious use of groundbait in the shape of whole or chopped up fish does definitely attract pike to a swim. Handfuls of whole sprats liberally thrown into a likely swim will usually bring results, although whole or chopped herrings are better, for the sprats attract far too many small pike, whereas the herring is more likely to lure the bigger fish into the swim. Unfortunately, groundbait of this type not only attracts the fish, but also feeds them as well. Because of this there is a good chance that the prowling pike will gorge themselves on the loose baits, and totally disregard a bait which has been carefully mounted on deadbait tackle. The answer is to use only limited numbers of fish as groundbait, and to make sure that the hook bait is as large and as fresh and attractive as possible. Pike will take half-decomposed fish baits, but seem to prefer a fresh deadbait when they can get it.

Deadbaiting with float tackle

Pike will take deadbaits on or off the bottom, and under certain circumstances a deadbait suspended a foot or two off

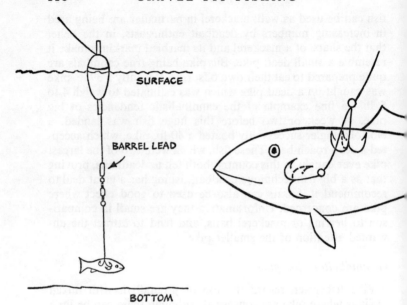

58. A: Float fished deadbait technique. B: Method of hooking float fished deadbait on snap tackle.

the bottom can be highly effective. On windy days when the water's surface is disturbed, a bait mounted on snap tackle (see fig. 58) so that it hangs below the float as naturally as possible will often produce more bites than a deadbait fished on leger tackle. This is probably due to the motion of the water which causes the bait to work up and down. This movement will occasionally attract a pike which would normally have ignored a static bait. The tackle should be set so that the bait hangs close to the pit bed, a bait fished at the mid-water level will seldom catch much.

Laying on with float tackle

This is a technique closely akin to the conventional leger tackle normally employed by deadbait users. The float serves no useful purpose other than that of a bite indicator, and because of this small floats are best, bearing in mind, however,

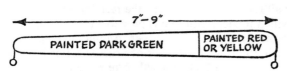

59. Balsa pencil float for laying on with deadbait.

that they have to remain visible even at extreme distances or in poor light. The ideal type of float to use is the kind used by bass and mackerel fishermen for float fishing in salt water. These have a long, slim body with a largish, brightly-coloured top (see fig. 59). Floats of this kind can be made at home from balsa wood or bought from any tackle stockist. These are normally made as sliders and should be used as such. In waters where the pike have learned to pick up a bait cautiously, a float is the ideal bite detector to use, for providing it is set to sit at half-cock on the water (see fig. 60), the slightest pull on the bait will be clearly registered. On standard leger tackle these initial pulls might well go completely unnoticed. The float leger is best used in water no more than 10 or 12 ft. in depth. Over this depth the tackle can become rather unmanageable. In swims which are thickly carpeted with weed, the float not only acts as a bite indicator but also keeps the line between terminal tackle and rod tip (see fig. 61) above the weed; with a standard leger, the line would quickly sink into the weed, which would make bite detection difficult and effective striking almost impossible.

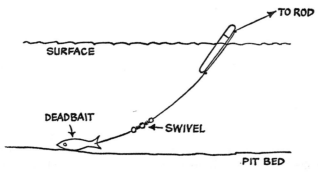

60. Float should be at half cock, when fished with laying on method.

For all forms of float fishing, the reel line should be rubbed over with a floatent. Musclin is probably the best, and is easily obtainable through a tackle dealer. An untreated line will sink and catch up on weed or other obstructions. For legering, untreated line should be employed. Pike sometimes pick up and drop a bait two or three times before attempting to take it properly. These preliminary bites usually cause the float to bob sharply. Under no circumstances should the tackle be touched or moved at this stage, for this will alarm the fish and cause it to drop the bait and vacate the area. If these rules are observed, the fish will gain confidence and take the bait firmly in its jaws and move off in the normal fashion, with the float

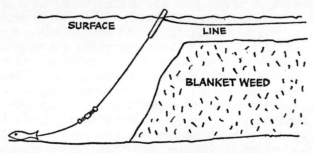

61. Float helps to keep line above weed.

sliding along the surface clearly indicating the direction in which the fish is moving. During the past season, I took three pike of over 20 lb. weight on float-fished deadbaits from a shallow gravel pit in Hampshire.

Legered deadbait

This is the simplest and best all-round method of deadbait fishing, a technique which is widely used by pike specialists all over the British Isles. Obviously a bait presented on leger tackle is intended to lie right on the pit bed. Consequently no float should be used, nor for that matter is a lead necessary, for the weight of the herring or mackerel bait is quite sufficient for casting purposes and a fresh, dead sea-fish will sink quickly to the bottom, for all the air will have been forced out of the swim bladder either in the nets, or during the packing process.

62. A marks deadbait's swim bladder. This in the case of freshly caught baits should be punctured with a baiting needle.

Freshly caught roach, rudd, etc., will float unless their swim bladders are broken. This is best achieved by running a baiting needle through the bladder area (see fig. 62). Probably the most important part of the deadbait tackle is the trace. This is normally made up as follows: first, take 2 ft. of wire or nylon-covered wire of 12 or 15 lb. b.s. Tie a single-barrel swivel to one end, and then slide a size 1 or 1-0 single-eyed hook and a single size 4 or 6 treble hook on to the wire. Finally, tie a treble of corresponding size to the loose end of the wire, and the trace is complete (see fig. 63). The bait should be mounted

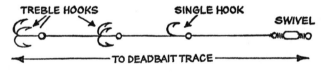

63. Wire deadbait trace.

so that it hangs head down with one treble on either side of its body. To do this the trace should be wound round the bait. The single hook should be inserted into the root of the bait's tail, and, if necessary, secured with two or three twists of copper wire. The bait is then ready for use (see fig. 64). By positioning a treble hook on each side of the bait's body, there is every chance that at least one hook will engage when the strike is made. The single hook serves no useful purpose except to hold the bait more securely during casting, for deadbaits are often rather soft and unless firmly attached to the

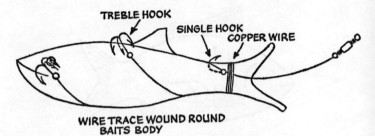

64. Wire traces wound round bait's body.

hooks may easily tear free in mid-air. Specimen hunters are now beginning to use a twist of strong paper in preference to the copper wire already mentioned, the idea being that the paper will be strong enough to hold the hook in place during casting, but when immersed in water will lose its strength and will in no way mar the strike. This is a new idea and one which could be used to great advantage by deadbait enthusiasts.

Balanced deadbait

Large deadbaits are comparatively heavy, and in pits which have a thick growth of blanket weed, the bait may well have a tendency to sink from sight into this weed. To overcome this, two buoyant strips of cork or, better still, polystyrene should be firmly lashed to either side of the deadbait's tail (see fig. 65). Trial and error will show just how much buoyancy should be added to a bait to make it balance correctly. A deadbait which is correctly balanced will sink slowly head first, and will

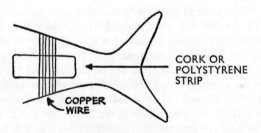

65. Detail of Fig. 64.

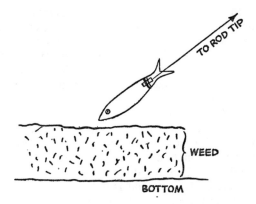

66. How a balanced deadbait appears to the pike.

come to rest on the weed, nose down (see fig. 66). This makes it appear like a naturally feeding fish and because of this the pike often take a bait fitted with buoyancy strips with confidence. To make the bait even more natural it should be mounted on the trace so that it hangs tail down instead of head down, as with the normal deadbait tackle. The single hook should be passed through both lips of the bait, with the two treble hooks spaced accordingly. This will leave the tail section of the bait looking as natural as possible, for the remainder of the trace and the reel line will lead away from the deadbait's head and be concealed by the weed fronds.

Cut baits

Most pike anglers use whole fish as deadbait, but some large pike have been caught on halved baits. The tail section of a herring is thought to be the best, and has accounted for several pike in excess of 25 lb. Being smaller than the whole bait, a sectional bait can be fished on less hooks. We do not know whether or not pike hunt to any extent by smell, but the oil exuded by the flesh of a cut herring must help to attract a hungry pike to the bait.

How to cast a very big bait

Big baits account for big fish, and pike are no exception to this rule. In consequence, specialist pike fishermen are beginning to use very big baits in an attempt to catch only the largest of pike. Baits weighing up to 2 lb. or more are ideal for this, and chub, bream and pike of this size make perfect baits. No normal rod could, of course, take the strain of casting baits as large as this, and consequently the bait should either be thrown out by hand, or, better still, with a casting pole (see fig. 67). When hand-throwing a bait, the rod should be first laid carefully in the rod rests, the reel pick-up opened so that the line can run freely from the spool, and the bait thrown out with an underarm motion. Great care should be taken to ensure that the projecting hook-points do not catch in the hand as the bait is projected. This method is only useful for fishing close to the bank, and if any distance is required, a casting pole is essential. This need not be elaborate, but should be long,

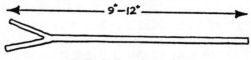

67. Forked casting pole.

supple, and forked at one end. Once again the rod should be in the rests and the reel pick-up opened before attempting to hurl the bait out. The bait should rest firmly but lightly in the fork of the pole; practice is required to achieve long throws with this set up, but once a degree of proficiency is obtained, casting will become simple.

Spinning

Pike respond well to shiny artificial baits, and a day's spinning can be a pleasant and rewarding pastime. As a general rule the average size of pike caught on artificial baits is low, but there have been plenty of very big pike caught on man-made lures. Pits that hold extensive stocks of pike make the best venues for the spin fisherman, for where pikes are prolific and have to compete with each other for food, sport can usually be relied upon, although even the most productive pike fisheries have their "off" days when nothing seems to interest the fish. One of the pleasantest things about spinning is that it keeps you on the move and allows you to cover a vast amount of water during the course of a day. Livebaiting and deadbaiting are static methods, and on a cold winter's day one can keep reasonably warm by walking round the pit casting the spoon bait into every likely pike lie. Spinning also allows one to travel light, with just a small shoulder bag to hold spare lures, food and a gaff or landing net clipped to the shoulder-bag strap.

Artificial lures are legion and many anglers tend to collect them. This is a mistake, for by carrying a vast selection of assorted artificial baits, there is a temptation to change over to a new bait after every few casts in a vain attempt to find a lure that will attract the pike. This is wrong for far too much time will be spent switching baits instead of fishing, and for this reason it is advisable to carry a small selection of carefully chosen practical lures. Fancy artificial baits can be extremely expensive and are no better fish-catchers than the plain, cheaper baits of the well tried and proved patterns. The best lures are usually made in Sweden, for the Swedish people have been making and using artificial lures for at least 200 years and have perfected the design of many basic baits. Silver-coloured lures work best in clear water, and copper-coloured baits are most effective in dirty, dark water. Because of this, it pays to carry two or three baits of each colour, or buy the baits that are finished with silver on one side and copper on the other.

Deep and slow is an adage often applied to pike spinning, and a very true one it is, for pike often refuse a bait that spins rapidly along at the mid-water mark, but will take it with confidence if it flashes slowly along close to the pit bottom. Extra movement can be imparted to the bait by raising or lowering the rod tip at irregular intervals, or by moving the rod tip from side to side. By slowing up the rate of retrieve or stopping it momentarily, the bait will pause or flutter down like a sick or wounded fish. This movement definitely adds to the attractiveness of the bait. Pike sometimes hook themselves when they take a spinner, but it is advisable to strike at any check to the forward motion of the bait.

Spinning with a natural bait

This is a popular method among Norfolk pike fishermen, but one that is seldom used by gravel pit anglers, despite the fact that a carefully-spun natural bait can be a deadly lure for pike of all sizes. Roach, dace, gudgeon, sprats and small herrings all make good natural spinning baits, although the freshly-killed fish are probably the best, for their flesh is still firm, whereas the flesh of the sea fish may well be soft, which means that it will tear off the hooks or break up completely in a very short space of time. Natural baits should be mounted on a specially constructed spinning flight or on wobbling tackle

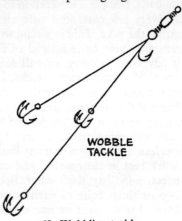

68. Wobbling tackle.

(see fig. 68). These, if used correctly, will impart just the right degree of spin or wobble to the dead fish. A wobbled natural bait is probably the better of the two methods, but both are highly effective. A wobbled bait should be worked very slowly across the pit bed, and should be allowed to settle to the bottom at regular intervals. This will often cause a following pike to pick up the bait, presumably thinking that in some way it has managed to kill the fish during the chase. This technique is similar in many respects to the straightforward deadbaiting methods described earlier. A pike will hang on to a spun natural bait far longer than an artificial lure, which gives more time to set the hooks.

8

ROACH

Many disused sand and gravel pits are capable of producing huge roach. This is particularly true of pits which have settled down and contain pure clear water, for roach seem to thrive best in pure water, probably because clean water is usually full of minute aquatic life, upon which the roach feed. Pits which are full of 4 to 6 oz. roach are unlikely to yield any fish of specimen side, for roach, like perch, are prolific breeders and quickly become stunted as a result of over-breeding. Pits which are likely to hold big roach seldom give up their secrets easily, although when a roach is caught from one of these waters it will usually be a big one. I discovered a pit of this type some years ago which was reputed to hold roach of 2 or 3 lb. in weight, although none had been caught for some years. I spent six months chasing these elusive fish for very mediocre results. Then during a heavy snow storm a roach of 2 lb. 8 oz. took my legered bait. This fish won me the sand and gravel award of the year for the best pit-caught roach of the season. Later in the year I went on to take other roach of specimen size from the same pit, but never in quantity, my best day's catch being made up of fourteen fish weighing between 1 lb. 8 oz. and 2 lb. 1 oz. I once took two fish from the water in two casts, both weighing 2 lb. $6\frac{1}{2}$ oz. Despite this promising start, not another fish or, for that matter, bite did I get for the rest of the day. Many expert roach anglers have spent a lifetime trying to catch a roach of over 2 lb. in weight, and even by today's high standard, roach of this weight are by no means common.

It is difficult to decide at what size a roach becomes a specimen, for there is much growth variation from one water to the next, but normally any roach weighing 1 lb. can be regarded as a good fish, and anything over $1\frac{1}{2}$ lb. as a specimen, a 2-pounder being a very big roach indeed. Modern tackle and methods have produced first-class results where roach are concerned, and roach specialists all over the country are taking 2 lb. plus specimens in ever increasing numbers. Many of these monsters fall to a small handful of dedicated anglers who devote a great deal of angling time to studying big roach and their movements. The average pit angler, however, is quite capable of catching a 2 lb. roach, providing first of all a suitable water is located and sufficient time is spent in pursuit of the larger fish. Like most aspects of specimen hunting, big roach fishing can be a slow and unproductive occupation, and many anglers turn to other fish after a blank weekend or two; only a determination to overcome all the many problems of catching specimen fish will produce consistently good results. Seemingly big roach should always be carefully examined, particularly if they are approaching record size, for roach often cross with rudd and bream, and although a big fish may have the appearance of a true roach there is always the possibility that it is in fact a hybrid and not a true roach at all. There have been a number of record or near-record roach recorded during the past few years, which when carefully examined by an expert have proved to be hybrid fish. Usually a careful examination of the fish will show slight differences; roach/rudd hybrids for instance are often deeper and a little more golden than true roach. The anal fin shape usually shows the difference between roach or roach/bream crosses, for the fin of the hybrid is more elongated than that of a true roach. If in doubt always get a second and, where possible, qualified opinion. This may mean killing the fish, a job which no true angler will relish, but a job which is essential if a near-record fish is to be positively identified. Big fish are of course usually nearing the end of their life span. This may be a comfort to any angler faced with making the decision to kill a very big and very beautiful fish. Where possible two scales should be taken from the shoulder of any big roach that are caught. These scales should then be submitted to a scale-reading expert, either through local angling officials or via the offices of an angling newspaper. From these scales an experienced icthyologist can determine the age and the growth rate of the fish. Information of this kind can be invaluable to both the angler who caught the fish and the owners of the pit from which it came. The 2 lb. 8 oz.

roach I caught from a sand pit in Kent was estimated to be ten or eleven years old, proving that the fish had grown fairly rapidly, and, more important still, that the fish in the pit in question were capable of reaching a weight of at least 3 lb., for roach can continue to grow until they reach an age of approximately fifteen years. As luck would have it, I never managed to get a bigger roach from the water, although on several occasions I was fortunate enough to watch huge roach swim quietly through my swim. These fish would, I am sure, have topped the 3 lb. mark, though it is extremely difficult to judge accurately the weight of fish seen in water. I can, however, remember clearly how big my best roach looked as it came into the net, and the free-swimming roach I saw later appeared to be far larger than my own fish when viewed from a similar position and distance. A roach equalling the British record was taken several years ago from a pit in the Midlands, and at the same period other fish of around 3 lb. in weight were caught from the same water.

It always amazes me that big fish of many species can live for years in a water without anyone suspecting their presence. The answer to this must lie with the tackle and tactics used by the average angler, for big fish are by no means foolish creatures, and heavy, badly-used tackle combined with bankside noise is usually more than enough to send any large fish frantic with fear. Even the larger species often inhabit a water without anyone realising it, and I have seen and even caught big carp, pike and perch from pits which were thought to be devoid of these species. Big roach, of course, have long been noted for their inbred cunning and it is rare for the average 'bottom' fisher to land a roach of anywhere near specimen proportions. Oddly enough, big roach can often be found in pits which contain a large head of decent-sized pike, for although the pike do eat vast amounts of roach, the fish that are left have an ample supply of food and may grow to a large size. I know of one very ancient pit in Hampshire which contains hundreds of pike, some of them topping the 30 lb. mark, catches of a dozen or more good pike are common and yet this pit also yields large bags of specimen roach to the patient and competent angler. This will probably surprise many of the anti-pike brigade, who are convinced that pike and other coarse fish simply will not mix, but it only goes to show that fish which are preyed upon by large predators often reach a good weight, simply because they are continually being weeded out. This is really nature's way of selective growing and as all the weak fish and many of the fry are destroyed in huge numbers the prime fish are given sufficient room to develop to the full.

FEEDING HABITS OF ROACH

Roach are generally regarded as a bottom-feeding species, but there are occasions when roach of all sizes will rise right up to the surface in search of food. This reversal of normal feeding pattern only occurs during hot weather when the oxygen content of the water is low, or when the surface of the water is thick with spent insect life upon which the roach can feed. The smaller roach are usually more prone to surface feeding than the big fish. Roach live for the most part on various types of insects, caddis grub, nymphs and larvae being the mainstay of their diet. They will also eat worms, weed, bread or cereal whenever these foods are available. River fishermen often catch big roach on the soft silkweed which grows on the woodwork of weirs and lock cuttings. Pit roach will also eat soft blanket weed in a similar fashion. They probably do this to get at the minute insect life which lives among this weed. In high summer roach can sometimes be caught from shallow water with their mouths and bellies distended with weed. Roach will also eat small water snails and tiny swan mussels. Very big roach occasionally show a predatory streak and more than one 2 lb. roach has taken a live minnow bait intended for perch. Many fish show these cannibalistic tendencies usually just after the spawning period when the water is thick with small fry. There is, however, little evidence to show that a tiny livebait will consistently catch roach.

BAITS FOR ROACH

Maggot

This is the most widely-used of all coarse-fishing baits and one of the most popular of all roach baits. The roach is predominately an insect eater which shows a marked preference for caddis grubs, which maggots closely resemble. As a bait, maggots are easily obtainable, reasonably cheap to purchase in quantity and clean to use. Loose maggots can also be used to 'groundbait' a swim. Although roach of all sizes will accept a hook baited with a large bunch of maggots, the bigger fish are more likely to accept a single or double maggot bait, as these look more natural than the bunched baits. Match anglers have bred a wide variety of maggots, many of which are dyed exotic colours, pink, red, lime, green and yellow being the most popular shades. Many matchmen are convinced that these unnaturally-coloured grubs are better fish catchers than the plain undyed maggot. This may be true when the bait is being used on heavily-fished waters where the fish have learned to associate the natural maggot with danger, but for pit fishing the naturally-coloured bait has no equal. To make the bait appear as natural as possible, the hook point should be passed just under the skin of the blunt end of the maggot (see fig. 69).

69. Maggot correctly hooked.

Under no circumstances should the maggot be threaded on to the hook. This not only destroys their natural appearance but ultimately kills them, and a dead maggot is practically useless as bait.

Worms

Few anglers realise that a lively redworm or brandling is one of the finest of all roach baits, consequently it is rare to see worms being used by roach fishermen. One of Britain's finest canal roach anglers, Mr Albert Oldfield, who is Bailiff on a stretch of the Macclesfield Canal, is a firm believer in worm baits, and uses huge lobworms to catch the big roach which live in the canal. His impressive score of 2 to 3 lb. roach is an example of the deadliness of worms as roach bait. My own largest roach was taken on a lively redworm and I have every confidence in worms where roach are concerned. The smaller worms appear to be most effective for pit roach fishing, possibly because pits often contain vast numbers of blood-worms which the small redworms closely resemble. I have, however, taken roach to 1 lb. 14 oz. on the tail end of a lob-worm (see fig. 70). When worm is used as bait, is it advisable

70. How to hook the tail of a lobworm.

to refrain from groundbaiting with whole worms, although a few chopped worms mixed in with mashed bread or bran groundbait can help to attract fish.

Bread baits

Roach are very fond of bread-based baits and will feed readily on crust, flake or paste. Crust and flake are soft baits which can be quickly torn from the hook. When using either of these baits it is essential to strike at the slightest indication of a bite, otherwise the fish will immediately suck the bait from the hook. Paste is a more substantial bait, which can be most effective. The best paste is made from the crumbs of a day-old loaf; this should be mixed with water and carefully kneaded to the right consistency in a clean cloth. Where possible, it is best to prepare paste at the waterside, for tap water often contains a chemical taint which may deter the fish. Heavy smokers will be well advised to wash their hands thoroughly in pit water before baiting up. Observing points like this can make all the difference to a day's fishing. Paste can be flavoured with honey, or coloured by introducing custard powder. At one time many anglers believed that various oils added to paste made the bait irresistible to the roach. There is, however, no proof to substantiate this belief, and of course there is no such thing as a secret bait. This may come as a surprise to the many average anglers who still believe in such things, but the fact remains that the man who continually catches good fish, irrespective of species, is simply a first-class angler who catches fish through skill and knowledge, not by using a secret bait as so many people believe.

Hempseed

For bulk catches of roach, hempseed is without doubt the most killing of all known roach baits. Hemp was originally introduced into this country by Belgian refugees just before or just after the start of the First World War, and has proved so deadly that many angling societies ban its use on their waters. Uncooked hempseed can be purchased from tackle dealers and pet shops. Jars of prepared and preserved hemp are also obtainable, but in my experience are worse than useless, as the preservative used seems to taint the bait so badly that roach will rarely feed on it. Before it can be used,

71. Bend of hook pushed into split in cooked hempseed grain.

the raw hemp must be boiled in a saucepan full of water until the individual grains split, showing the white kernel of the seed. Once this occurs the water should be strained off through a piece of muslin, and the hemp left to cool. The cooling process can be hastened by washing the seed under the cold tap. Once cool, the hemp should be placed in a bait tin or, better still, a linen bag. Never prepare hempseed more than twenty-four hours in advance, for the seed has a tendency to go sour if left unused for two or three days. Sour bait will, of course, catch no fish. By adding a dash of soda to the boiling water the hemp can be darkened, which may make it more attractive to the fish. When baiting up with hemp, the hook bend should be pushed gently into the crack in the seed (see Fig. 71); never thread the seed on to the hook, for this will mar the penetration of hook point when the strike is made. Hempseed can also be prepared by putting it into a thermos flask of boiling water and leaving it to stand overnight. Occasionally, however, this method will overcook the hemp, making it too soft to use.

Stewed wheat

This is quite a good roach bait but is rather out of fashion these days. Wheat should be stewed until fairly soft, the thermos flask technique mentioned in the section on hempseed being the ideal way of preparing this cereal for use. Roach have to be attracted to wheat by consistent groundbaiting. Roach seldom become preoccupied with wheat, although when a large shoal locates the groundbaited swim, sport can often be good.

Other roach baits

Tinned peas make quite good roach baits, although heavy groundbaiting is essential before the roach can be expected to accept a bait of this kind. Cheese cubes are a first-class but little-used bait. These are often effective on waters where the roach treat more conventional baits with caution. Cheddar or processed cheese is best. Cheese can also be mixed into bread paste. Roach presumably come to this bait because of its smell. Tiny portions of chopped swan mussel (see Tench chapter) make good roach baits, particularly when the swim has been heavily groundbaited with pieces of mussel. Almost any bankside grub or insect can be used to catch roach, these only being used as a last resort when other baits are unobtainable.

LOCATION OF ROACH

Unlike bream, roach seldom give away their whereabouts by rolling or priming on the surface, consequently a period of trial and error is often required to locate a swim which the roach shoals visit regularly. Deepish gravelly-bottomed swims, particularly those which have shallow water on either side (see fig. 72), often produce good catches, and shallow water swims close to thick growths of soft bottom weed are also likely places to try, for the weed is almost certain to contain a multi-

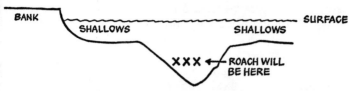

72. Deep gravelly-bottomed holes close to shallow water are ideal places to find big pit roach.

tude of insect life which acts as a natural groundbait. Deep holes close to sheltered areas of pit bank often fish well, especially in the late evening when the roach shoals move out of the rapidly cooling shallows and begin to drop back into the deeper water. Beds of surface weed never seem to attract roach to any great extent, although beds of sunken lilies, or 'cabbage patches' as they are usually called, are often ideal places to find and catch big roach. In the winter, the roach seldom venture far from deep water and unless there has been a prolonged period of mild weather, the winter roach angler will be well advised to concentrate on the deeper swims. Like many other pit fish, roach are often attracted to feeder streams and seem to delight in the play of the running water.

TACKLE FOR ROACH

There are dozens of rods available to the roach angler, most of which are quite suitable for general roach fishing. For float fishing in deepish pits, a long rod is advisable. This can be made of hollow glass or split cane and should have an easy action. This means that the rod should be supple enough to cast a light float a fair distance and pliable enough to pick up long line when the strike has to be made. Match-type rods which are constructed so that all the action is concentrated into the last 18 in. are of little use to the pit angler, for they are designed for fast, under-the-rod-tip striking at small fish. For this sort of work they are perfect, but for hooking and playing very large roach they are practically useless. The ideal roach rod is between 12 and 14 ft. in length, although for the shorter angler, an 11 to 12 ft. rod may be more comfortable. The

same rod can also be used for light leger work, although a
MKIV Avon rod is more practical for this kind of fishing.

Reels

Although a centre-pin reel is quite useful for fishing the
bankside swims, a fixed-spool reel is a more versatile reel,
and for general fishing is unsurpassed.

Lines

Fine lines are essential for roach fishing, and for float fishing
a line with a 3 or 4 lb. b.s. is the heaviest that should be used,
except when fishing weedy or snagged-up swims, when a line
with a 5 or even 6 lb. b.s. may have to be employed. It is
noticeable that when a heavier line is used there is a sharp
decline in the number of bites received per session. This is
understandable, for big roach are line-shy fish and will eject
a suspect bait at the slightest indication that all is not as it
should be.

Hooks

Roach have small mouths and show a general preference for
small baits; in consequence it is advisable to choose one's
hooks carefully. For hempseed, single maggot or other very
small baits, a size 16 hook is best; for bread wheat or bunched
maggot baits, sizes 12 to 14 are most suitable; and for worms,
a size 8 or 10 hook should be used, depending upon the size of
the worm. Round bend hooks with fine points are best for
roach fishing; whether or not one buys loose-eyed hooks or
hooks tied to a length of nylon is purely a matter of personal
choice. For most fish I prefer to buy eyed hooks and tie them
directly to the reel line, but for roach I prefer to use the tied
to nylon variety, mainly because hooks of this kind are neatly
tied and sharp, moreover the round bend types are readily
available, whereas it is difficult to obtain hooks of this shape
in the eyed variety, except in very well-stocked tackle shops,
which are unfortunately very few and far between.

Floats

Goose, porcupine or peacock quills make beautiful roach

floats. These are obtainable from any tackle shop, but are unfortunately usually highly varnished. This flashiness may be attractive to the human eye, but can be very off-putting where fish are concerned, for this reason it is advisable to paint over the lower section of the float with a matt green or brown paint. In rough water, an antennae float is the best type to use, for these floats are designed to ride steadily in the most disturbed water. These floats can be easily made up at home from a suitable length of dowling and a length of lightweight paper (see fig. 73); cork, balsa, or polystrene can also be used,

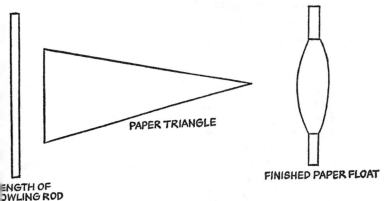

PAPER TRIANGLE

FINISHED PAPER FLOAT

LENGTH OF
DOWLING ROD

73. How to make paper floats.

but these materials require a lot of work to shape and finish. The paper method gives a good body shape and can be quickly waterproofed with balsa dope or Durofix glue. For fishing deep water, extra-long floats should be used. These are more sensitive and have more stability. Whenever possible a roach float should be attached by the bottom end only. This makes the float more sensitive.

Weights

When float-fishing, split shot and lead wire should be used to cock the float. For leger work, small arlsey bombs make the best pattern weights. Coffin leads, and drilled bullets should be avoided, for they are cumbersome, awkward leads, which seldom slide freely on the line.

METHODS OF CATCHING ROACH

Float fishing

The present roach record was taken on a float leger (see fig. 74), but nowadays this type of terminal tackle is seldom

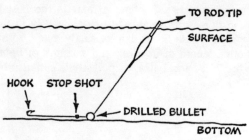

74. Float leger.

used, for although it is quite effective, it is not quite as sensitive as the true leger. This method can, however, be useful when used in deep water, for providing the float is set correctly the slightest bite will be clearly indicated. A sliding float, with the line running freely through the bottom ring, is the most convenient and sensitive float to use in deep water. The float should be stopped at the correct distance from the weight by a tiny segment of rubber band tied securely on to the line.

General float fishing

Roach live and feed close to the bottom, consequently light float tackle, set so that the bait just trips or lays on the pit bed (see fig. 75) can be used to good effect while roach fishing. Only the lightest of floats should be used, for roach will seldom take a bait suspended beneath a heavy float. Quills are ideal, but cork or balsa-bodied floats can be used providing that the size of the body is kept within reasonable bounds. For fishing deep pits which are open to the wind, a double-bodied float (see fig. 76) can be most useful. The stability of this type of float is extremely good, and even in the strongest of winds these floats can be relied upon to remain steady. This is very important, for a bait which continually bobs up and down will catch few fish. Twin-bodied floats can be bought from many tackle shops.

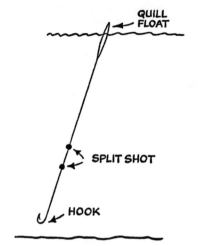

75. Off the bottom roach tackle.

76. Double ended float.

Whipping for roach

On hot, sultry evenings, roach of all sizes often rise to the surface of the water in search of insect food, and judicious groundbaiting with handfuls of maggots or chrysalis will usually lure the fish to within easy casting-range of the bank. Under these circumstances the normally cautious roach often lose their shyness completely, and providing regular quantities of groundbait are continually introduced into the swim, large bags of prime fish can be caught. It is advisable to spend an hour or so drawing the fish into the swim before attempting to actually fish. This will ensure that the roach have time to become preoccupied with the groundbait before they realise the presence of the angler. Once the fish are feeding confidently on the surface, it is very difficult to make them go off the feed again.

There are several ways of catching surface-feeding roach, one being to fish with a self-cocking float set only a few inches deep (see Rudd chapter), the other being to whip or free-line fish. This is an interesting and highly productive technique, which has much in common with orthodox fly-fishing. A flexible easy-action rod is essential, and the reel line should be greased with line floatant, leaving only the last 12 or 15 in. of line nearest the hook untreated. This will allow the bait to sink slowly down in a natural fashion (see fig. 77). Practice

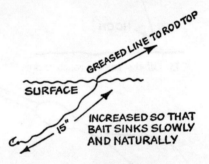

77. Greased line.

is required to cast a single maggot or chrysalis bait on this tackle, but it is not a difficult art to master, for the spring of the rod will help you to propel the bait. The secret of this form of fishing is to lure the fish to you, and then fish with as short a line as possible. Bites on free-line tackle can be expected from the moment the bait hits the water; the fish seem unable to differentiate between the hook bait and the natural bait and will usually bite most decisively. Very often it is possible to watch the fish actually take the bait, but the easiest method of bite detection is to watch the greased line that is floating on the water, as soon as this begins to tighten or slide off across the surface the strike should be made. Very few bites will be missed with free-line tackle, for the roach take the bait with the utmost confidence. By the continual feeding of groundbait into the swim, the roach shoals can be kept condensed into a comparatively small area, and as each fish has to compete with others for the bait they will seldom show the cautious approach that is normally associated with big roach. This technique gets its name of whipping from the rod movement that is required to cast the bait.

Fishing below the main shoal

Although the above method can be extremely effective with medium-sized roach, the extra-large fish sometimes refuse to be drawn right to the top of the water, and content themselves with swimming about below the main shoal, picking up any odd scraps of food which are overlooked by the smaller fish. The only practical method of catching these extra-big, ultra-cautious roach is to pinch a small shot on to the line close to the bait so that the bait sinks rapidly through the ranks of the medium roach. This often works well, and a tiny fragment of cork should be clipped on to the line so that although the bait can drop for several feet it finally finishes up suspended among the larger fish. The cork fragment acts both as a support for the bait and as a bite indicator. If a bite is not registered within a minute or two, the tackle should be drawn back so that the bait rises towards the surface. A 6 in. pull will be enough to do this. Once the tackle has been moved in this way, the bait should be allowed to drift down again. Roach seem to find this movement most attractive.

Fishing with hempseed

Roach of all sizes love to feed on hempseed, and on many waters where hemp is consistently used the resident roach shoals become so addicted to this seed that they will often ignore all other baits completely. Because of this, some angling clubs stipulate in their rule books that no angler shall use this deadly bait. On pits where the use of hempseed is permissible, a day's 'hemping' can be most productive, although far from relaxing, for bites on hempseed are normally very fast affairs which require complete concentration and co-ordination to connect with; even an expert hemp fisherman is lucky to hook one in three bites, and the average angler trying hemp for the first time will completely miss at least three-quarters of the bites indicated by the float. The reflex striking action of the expert takes time to develop, but constant practice will soon perfect the striking technique. In waters where hemp is regularly used, very little groundbait will be required to attract the roach shoals, but on waters where hemp is a comparatively new bait, it may be necessary to feed the swim regularly with loose grains of seed. Once the fish begin to feed, the quantity of groundbait should be gradually decreased so that the fish have to hunt for their food. It is advisable, however, to throw out a few grains of hemp every time a fish is

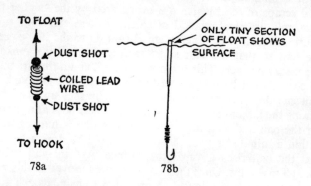

hooked. This will stop the shoal from breaking up. By doing this religiously it is usually possible to hold the shoal in one concentrated area for as long as is required; without the groundbait the shoal will quickly become alarmed by the disturbances created by the hooked fish and disperse. Once this occurs it may take hours to re-group the shoal in the swim.

Once the fish are right on feed, they will take anything that vaguely resembles a grain of hemp. Split shot, of course, comes into this category, and if shot are used to cock the float, many false bites will be registered. To overcome this, a small coil of lead wire, stopped at either end by a dust shot, should be used as a weight (see fig. 78a), the shot being placed right against the wire, so the whole weight becomes a neat compact package. For extra sensitivity, the float should be attached by the bottom end only, and weighted so that only a tiny section projects above the surface (see fig. 78b). This is most important, for hemp bites are very sharp and, unless the float is well ballasted, many of the bites received will barely make the float dip. If the tackle is set properly, however, each bite will pull the float completely under the water, making bite detection far simpler. Tiny quill floats are best for hemping, a 3 in. length of peacock quill being easily as sensitive as the more elaborate floats on the market, and costing a fraction of the price.

When the roach are feeding a small section of valve rubber can be used as bait in place of the usual grain of hemp. The roach seem unable to differentiate between the rubber and the real thing. The rubber can be used over and over again, for the fish will be unable to pull it off the hook. Much fishing time can be saved by using a substitute bait of this kind, as there will be no necessity to re-bait after each successive bite. It may be necessary to alter the distance between float and hook on a number of occasions while hemp fishing, for shoaling roach have a tendency to change their feeding-levels fairly frequently. A cessation of regular bites indicates that the fish have done this, and that the tackle needs adjustment. It occasionally pays to fish right on the bottom when hemp fishing, for the very big roach will sometimes accept a bait fished in this way, while ignoring one fished in the conventional manner.

There is a lot of absolute nonsense talked about the harm hemp is supposed to do, for hemp fed roach are usually in the peak of condition. Many anglers still believe that the bait is a drug, and also that uneaten hemp grains have a tendency to ferment on the bottom and pollute the water. There is absolutely nothing to back up these theories, which unfortunately are widely believed. I have even heard hemp being blamed for a disease called black spot which seems to attack roach more than any other fish. This again is rubbish, for it has been established that this disease is caused by bird-droppings which fall into the water. Anglers are notoriously dogmatic, however, and once an idea is implanted in their minds it is very difficult to get them to change their views. Because of this hemp should only be used in pits where no one objects to its use. No one quite knows why roach take hemp so well, but there is the theory that it bears a resemblance to a small water snail upon which the roach feed. Other cereal baits can be used but seem to lack the deadliness of the hemp.

Night fishing

Like many fish, roach are semi-nocturnal and will feed well throughout the night. Carp anglers are often bothered by roach of specimen size which somehow manage to swallow huge balls of bread paste. Oddly enough, few anglers deliberately fish for roach at night, although those that do are often rewarded with first-class catches. My experience of night fishing for big roach has been rather limited, but I have caught some big roach after dark, including fish of 2 lb. 2½ oz. and 2 lb. 1 oz. During the warmer months the roach shoals often venture into shallow water during the night. Because of this it is advisable to concentrate on swims of medium depth. A plain running leger should be used in clear swims, and a link-on wooden leger in weedy ones (see fig. 79). Flake from

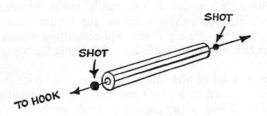

79. Drilled out wooden leger weight.

the inside of a new loaf seems to make the best bait, but crust can also be used to good effect. Few anglers ever consider night fishing after the end of September, but big roach often feed well during the early part of a winter night. This seems to apply particularly to pit roach. The air temperatures often rise slightly as darkness falls and this rise of temperature often brings the roach shoals on feed. During the colder months, the roach seldom wander far from the deeper areas of a pit, and most of the big roach I have caught while fishing on winter nights have been caught in swims which were 12 to 15 ft. in depth. Pit roach seem to dislike mud and silt, and the ideal swim is one which has a bottom composed of clean gravel. Winter roach also prefer to feed just off the bottom, consequently float tackle is more likely to catch fish than leger tackle.

There are, of course, exceptions to this rule, but my own personal experiences lead me to believe that float fishing is the superior technique. Obviously it is not possible to watch a float in the dark, and a bite indicator is essential. A fold of silver paper twisted over the line between the first and second rod ring is ideal (see fig. 80), for being practically weightless

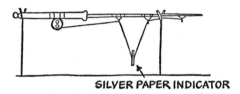

SILVER PAPER INDICATOR

80. Silver paper indicator.

it does not alarm a taking fish. Large floats should never be used. A quill or tiny antennae float is most suitable. For deep-water work, a sliding float should be used. This will simplify the casting problem, and allow bites to be struck directly. Fixed floats tend to cushion the force of the strike and may lose you the roach of a lifetime. The tackle should be set so that the bait is suspended 6 to 9 in. off the bottom. Maggots, bread and worms make the best baits, a single maggot being particularly deadly. Bites are normally bold affairs, for the fish seem to lose their cautiousness after dark and will often take the bait boldly, causing the bite indicator to streak up to the rod rings. Bites like this are difficult to miss providing a careful watch is kept on the indicator.

Winter days are short, and by staying on at the waterside until eight or nine o'clock at night some extraordinarily good fishing can be had without too much personal discomfort. After about nine o'clock, however, the temperature starts to drop rapidly and once this happens the fish normally stop feeding. Not every angler will relish the prospect of spending a few after-dark hours at the waterside during the winter months, but for the man who wants to catch big roach these hours can make a great deal of difference to both the quantity and the quality of the roach he catches.

9

RUDD

Rudd are primarily still-water fish which thrive extremely well in wet pits of all kinds. Many writers have referred to the rudd as the golden fish of the lakes, and a better description could not be found, for a big rudd is a beautiful golden-bronze fish whose bright crimson fins set off the golden sheen of its flanks to perfection, making it a living jewel of unbelievable beauty. There is a variety of rudd which can occasionally be caught from waters which hold the more normal specimens. These fish, though golden in colour, have lemon-coloured fins instead of crimson ones. Why, or how, this variation occurs I cannot say, but I have caught quite a number of these lemon-finned rudd from various waters, and can only presume that they are comparatively common. Amateur anglers often confuse rudd with roach; this is understandable for both fish are rather similar in basic appearance. The simplest method of identification is to look at the mouth of the fish. If the lower lip recedes, it is a roach; if the lip projects, it is a rudd. Also, the lips of the true rudd are darker in colour than those of a roach. There are, of course, hybrids between the two species (see Roach chapter). Rudd grow to a slightly larger size than roach, and the rod-caught record weighed $4\frac{1}{2}$ lb. Any rudd over 2 lb. in weight can be regarded as a specimen, and those of over 3 lb. weight as outstanding fish.

Rudd, like roach, are unfortunately prolific breeders and, unless kept in check, will reproduce at such a rate that they soon overrun a pit, with the result that they totally exhaust the food supply of the water, and become stunted. Fish that do this are quite capable of breeding, but seldom reach a length of more than a few inches and are therefore useless as stock fish or as a sporting proposition, and are best removed from the water. I have known of a number of fine pits which have been completely ruined by the introduction of rudd as stock fish. On many carefully controlled pits rudd are totally barred from the water, even as livebait. Long-established pits which are rich in insect life and contain only a limited number of rudd are the places to fish if you wish to catch rudd of specimen proportions. The Landbeach pits in Cambridgeshire, for instance, are noted for the size and quality of the rudd they contain. These big fish, however, are few and far between, and consequently they don't have to compete with each other for particles of food, and are able to reach a large size. There are other similar pits in many parts of the country, and the dedicated rudd expert should be prepared to travel in search of good fish. I once caught eighteen rudd of over 2 lb. in weight in one sitting. This is an achievement which I never expect to repeat, for rudd of this size and in such quantity are rarely encountered. Despite their deep, powerful build, rudd are rather delicate fish, quick to die if confined for any great length of time in a keep-net. Rudd also seem prone to fungoid diseases which are, to some extent, contagious. Because of this any rudd caught should be handled with great care.

TACKLE FOR RUDD

Standard roach tackle can be used for most aspects of rudd fishing.

FEEDING HABITS OF RUDD

The rudd is essentially a surface-feeding fish which obtains much of its food from the underside of floating weed pads, or from submerged reed stalks. On warm evenings, when the rudd are feeding right off the surface, the loud sucking noises they make with their mouths can be used to locate the shoals. Big rudd occasionally feed right on the bottom like roach. This usually only occurs in shallow water, or during the winter months.

BAITS FOR RUDD

All the usual roach baits can be used to take rudd, but for the bigger fish large worms or big pieces of bread bait make the best baits. Small rudd can make a considerable nuisance of themselves, and the only way to overcome this problem is to use a very big bait which the smaller fish will be unable to swallow. Pieces of flake the size of a walnut are by no means too big for large rudd to take, for these fish seem to be able to open their mouths far wider than roach of similar size. Maggots can also be used as bait, but, being small, they attract the attention of the smaller fish which are more active and less discerning than the bigger rudd, and will usually rush at a maggot bait the moment it hits the surface of the water. The larger fish seldom get the opportunity to do this, for their bulk slows them down.

Bigg rudd show a more pronounced predatory streak than roach, and can often be caught on tiny livebaits or small, shiny, artificial lures. In Ireland, where rudd are probably the commonest coarse fish, local anglers use tiny rudd to catch big rudd and, in some areas, livebait is considered to be the best bait that can be obtained. I have caught rudd of specimen size on fly spoons on several occasions, but few British anglers as yet seem to livebait or spin for rudd, although on the Continent, particularly in Holland, roach, rudd and bream anglers regard spinning as a standard technique. These Continental anglers catch large numbers of big fish on spinning tackle, and have developed a special technique to take bream, roach, rudd and hybrids. Ultra-light tackle is used for this type of fishing. Tiny glass spinning rods, minute fixed-spool reels and 1 lb. b.s. lines are used as a matter of course. The artificial lures used are tiny delicate little baits, designed mainly on the bar-spoon principle, the treble hook being hidden by a tuft of red wool. These baits are obviously intended to look like roach or rudd fry, which backs up the theory that both these fish have cannibalistic tendencies. The method of fishing these little lures is rather interesting as well, and these baits seem to work best when fished over a clear bottom close to, or in between, thick beds of weed. Having selected a suitable swim, the Continental angler casts out, waits for the bait to touch the bottom and then begins to retrieve it fairly rapidly. After a yard or two of line has been wound back on to the reel spool, the bait is allowed to flutter down to the bottom, where it is left for anything up to five minutes before the whole process is repeated. Bites are most likely to occur when the bait is stationary, proving that not only are the roach, rudd and bream predatory, but that they are also scavengers that are willing to pick up and eat any small dead fish that come their way. I have used a similar technique to catch pit perch (see Perch chapter) but have yet to use this method for other coarse fish. On the Continent this technique is regarded as deadly, and there can be no real reason why British coarse fish should not respond equally well to it. To the best of my knowledge, however, no one has ever experimented along those lines in home waters, and consequently no one can say how effective this technique could be. It is, however, well worth a try and might lead to some exciting discoveries.

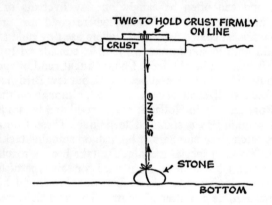

81. The anchored crust method of groundbaiting.

Groundbait

Being basically surface feeders, rudd do not respond at all well to normally prepared groundbait which is designed to sink quickly to the bottom. Even lightly mixed cloudbait, which breaks up as soon as it hits the surface and forms a cloud of slowly-sinking bait particles, will seldom hold the attention of the rudd for any appreciable length of time. There are only two simple, but practical, groundbaiting techniques; these are the dry bran method, which can only be used to groundbait corner swims into which the prevailing wind is blowing, and the anchored crust method (see fig. 81) which can be used in any swim, irrespective of wind or other climatic conditions.

The dry groundbait method of attracting rudd

Small quantities of dry groundbait poured directly into wind-ruffled water will quickly spread and form a wide patch or floating bait particles. By the pouring of several pounds of groundbait into the water, a very large surface area can be covered with a film of bait which will attract, and hold the attention of the rudd shoals without actually feeding them. By using light float tackle set so that the bait is suspended just beneath the surface it is possible to catch large numbers of rudd as they swim just beneath the film of floating groundbait.

The anchored crust method of attracting rudd

There is nothing new about this technique, for it has been used for years by Norfolk Broads rudd experts. It is, however, a most useful method of concentrating the rudd shoals into a relatively small area. There is nothing complicated about this anchored crust method; the bait is a thick piece of stale or toasted breadcrust tied to a length of string to which a stone or iron bolt has been attached, this weight serving to anchor the crust in the swim. To allow for drift, it is essential to determine accurately the depth of the swim, and allow an extra 18 in. of string between anchor weight and crust. If the string between weight and crust is too taut, the buoyancy of the bread will lift the weight and cause the whole lot to drift out of the swim. Under no circumstances should nylon be used as an anchor line, for nylon is practically invisible both in and out of the water, and a loose length of nylon may kill or maim a water bird. Worse still, nylon does not rot, consequently it can kill over and over again. Once the rudd begins to nuzzle at the crust, light float tackle baited with bread, worm or maggot can be cast directly at the crust so that the bait falls naturally, among the hungry fish.

LOCATION OF RUDD

Rudd shoals seldom venture far from cover, and the best

rudd swims are usually situated close to beds of lily or other thick weed. Bankside swims beneath overhanging trees are also likely to hold rudd, for a great deal of insect life will drop from the overhanging foliage into the water below, and rudd, like most fish, are quick to take advantage of a free supply of food. Even the tiniest patch of surface weed will attract rudd, particularly in the late evenings when the fish begin to rise steadily for the insects that hatch from beneath the leaves of the water weed. In clear pits, where there are no weed beds or tree-shaded swims, the rudd shoals can usually be located on the sunken sand bars and banks which usually divide the deep and shallow water.

METHODS OF CATCHING RUDD

Rudd, being surface, or semi-surface feeders, float tackle should be used to support the bait in the water. Like roach, rudd are shy fish and, where possible, only the lightest of tackle should be used. Self-cocking floats are best for rudd fishing (see fig. 82), for rudd are quick to shy away from a

LEAD WIRE WOUND
ROUND BASE OF QUILL

82. Commercially produced plastic float with hollow bottom section designed to hold split shot.

line which has a string of split shot attached to it. Also, a bait presented on self-cocking float tackle will sink at a natural speed, which in turn will attract the attention of the rudd. A useful tip when rudd are known to be in the swim but are refusing to bite is to slowly reel the tackle in a foot or two at a time. Rudd seem to be fascinated by a slowly moving bait and will often accept a bait fished in this way, yet will refuse to look at the same bait if hanging stationary in the water. This interest in moving baits may be another indication of the rudd's semi-predatory habits which were mentioned earlier in the bait section.

Winter rudd

Many anglers believe that rudd are exclusively a summer fish which disappear completely during the colder months. This is, of course, nonsense, for rudd remain active throughout the winter, but move from their summer haunts to deeper water where they often intermingle with the roach shoals. Rudd also tend to lose their golden-bronze colour during the winter, and turn silver instead. This makes them look very similar to roach, which is probably one reason why anglers believe that rudd only feed during warm weather and hibernate throughout the winter. When the water temperatures are low, the rudd shoals usually feed on, or close to, the bottom. Sport is at best spasmodic during the winter time, but rudd will occasionally feed well at midday when the light is at its brightest. These fish will also feed after dark, and can be caught on similar tackle to roach (see Roach chapter, section on night fishing). Winter rudd are in the peak of condition and can be relied upon to fight well when hooked.

Rudd on leger

Although rudd are usually fished for with float tackle, they can also be caught on a running leger, the leger being useful for fishing over areas of shallow water which are beyond casting range of float tackle.

Fly fishing for rudd

During periods of warm, settled weather, when the rudd shoals are actively engaged in hunting for spent insects on the surface of the water, the careful use of a dry-fly fishing outfit will produce plenty of action. Any light trout fly rod can be used for this game, the cheap, but light, hollow-glass fly rods are ideal. The rod should be used in conjunction with a cheap metal centre-pin reel, and a plain level fly line. More expensive tackle can be used, but most anglers will only use a fly rod on odd occasions, and for obvious reasons will probably wish to keep the cost of such an outfit to the absolute minimum. A suitably tapered nylon cast can be purchased in any tackle shop, as can a few well-dressed flies. Dark, hackled flies make the best lures, but winged flies can be used as well.

Providing no attempt is made to cast a long length of line, the techniques of general fly casting can soon be mastered. Constant practice and strict attention to timing is essential, but once the method is learnt it will never be forgotten. Rudd are bold risers and will take a fly in a decisive manner which can be most exciting. Moreover, a big rudd on a light fly rod can be relied upon to put up a grand fight, and for sheer fun, fly fishing for rudd when the fish are really on feed cannot be equalled.

Rudd bites on float tackle

Rudd of all sizes take a bait in a most characteristic way, causing the float to dip and bob before it finally begins to zig-zag off beneath the surface. There can be no mistaking a true rudd bite and yet, despite the ample indication the fish give as they take the bait, it is easy enough to miss the bite completely by striking too early. Practical experience will soon show that the best time to strike is when the fish is towing the tackle steadily along, and not during the first preliminary pulls, when the fish are taking and rejecting the bait rapidly. Roach anglers will find it difficult to control their reflexes when rudd fishing, for roach are sharp biters which often only make the float dip for a fraction of a second before dropping the bait.

10

TENCH

Tench are common in many pits, where they provide first-class sport for the summer angler. The present record rod-caught tench was taken from a gravel pit near Hemingford Gray in Huntingdonshire, and many tench of specimen size are taken from similar man-made waters during most seasons. Whether or not the record tench weight of 9 lb. 1 oz. will ever be beaten remains to be seen, but there is strong evidence to show that tench of over 10 lb. in weight do exist in certain gravel pits. At least one pit at Wraysbury in Middlesex holds tench of record size and, although I have no first-hand knowledge of the waters, I am told that record tench also exist in pits situated in the Midlands. Tench vary considerably in colour from one water to another, but are normally a beautiful golden bronze, or greeny-bronze colour. The eyes of the tench are red. Two very beautiful variations also occur: these are the golden tench (see Unusual Fish chapter) and the extremely rare vermilion tench. Both are originally ornamental fish, which have reverted to the wild state. Tench are powerful sporting fish which are immensely popular with pit anglers. Unfortunately the productive tench fishing season is comparatively short, the best sport being had during June and July. The fish also become active again in September. During October, the tench sink into a torpid state, or go into complete hibernation for the duration of the winter months. Very occasionally tench can be caught during periods of bright winter weather, and there has been much speculation in recent years as to whether or not winter tench fishing is a worthwhile occupation. Results have shown, however, that the wise tench angler will look to other fish to provide sport during the winter time, for at best tench will only feed spasmodically during the colder months and are hardly worth pursuing.

FEEDING HABITS OF TENCH

Tench are primarily bottom feeders and live mainly on the larvae of aquatic insects, small swan mussels and water snails. Very occasionally tench rise to the surface and suck down spent flies, and at the spring lake pits near Camberley a number of tench have been taken on artificial flies intended for trout.

BAITS FOR TENCH

Tench baits are legion, but for consistent success the tench angler will be well advised to fish with worm or bread baits, both of which make first-class tench lures. Large pieces of chopped swan mussel flesh is another popular tench bait. Swan mussels can be easily gathered by raking the pit bottom close to the bank with a fine-toothed rake (see fig. 83). Maggots

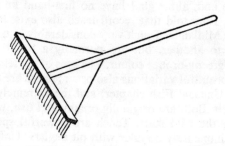

83. Fine-toothed swan mussel rake.

have accounted for a great many large tench, and in waters where there are no small fish, maggots can be used to good effect. Bread can be used in several forms, paste and flake being deadly big tench baits.

LOCATION OF TENCH

Tench occasionally disclose their whereabouts by rolling on the surface, but more often than not the angler will be forced to locate these fish by trying each likely-looking swim until tench are caught. Tench show a marked liking for heavy weed, and swims adjacent to lily beds are well worth fishing. During the early part of the season the shallowest swims are often the most productive. Later, as the season advances, the fish have a tendency gradually to work back into deeper water. Hungry tench are active fish which spend a good deal of time rooting about on the bottom, and while thus occupied, they send up clouds of frothy bubbles which show the observant angler just where to fish. Bubbling tench can usually be induced to take a bait; worm is particularly effective when tench are 'bubbling' in this fashion.

TACKLE FOR TENCH

Tench are strong game fish which fight extremely well when hooked. Because of this it is advisable to use fairly powerful tackle when tench fishing.

Rods

Match and light bottom-fishing rods are practically useless for tench fishing, and for all-round work a split cane or hollow-glass 11 or 12 ft. Avon-type trotting rod is ideal, for the easy progressive action of this kind of rod is used to the fullest extent while playing big tench. For legering, a slightly shorter rod can be used, the now famous MKIV Avon being a first-class weapon for tench catching.

Reels

When float-fishing bankside swims, a good quality centre-pin reel can be used for tench fishing. This kind of reel gives slightly more direct control over a hooked fish, and if used properly can be a pleasure to fish with. Fixed-spool reels are more practical for legering or long-range work.

Lines

Many big tench have been taken on ultra-light lines by expert anglers, but most fishermen will be well advised to use a line with a b.s. of at least 5 lb. while tench fishing. In thickly-weeded swims a 7 lb. b.s. line should be used, for there is little point in using a fine line if breakages are inevitable.

Hooks

Tench have leathery mouths which afford a good hook purchase, but strong hooks are essential, for tench are heavy fish which can easily distort a hook constructed from thin gauge wire. Short shank-eyed Model Perfect or standard goldstrike hooks, size 4, 6, 8 and 10, are the most useful hooks for tench fishing. Both are however rather thick in the wire, and should be sharpened carefully before use with a jeweller's file or fine carborundum stone.

Floats

Tench are sensitive fish which are prone to drop a bait if they suspect that there is anything unnatural about it, and because of this only the most delicate floats should be used. Quills are ideal, and light-bodied antennae floats are useful when fishing on windy days.

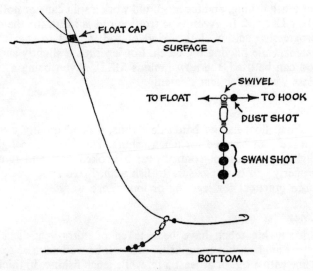

84. The swan shot float leger in use.

METHODS OF CATCHING TENCH

The swan shot float leger (see fig. 84)

Float legering has always been a popular method with bottom fishermen, but the old-fashioned float leger which employed a small drilled bullet weight is far from suitable where tench are concerned. The swan shot float leger, on the other hand, if properly adjusted in the first place, is an extremely sensitive set-up which will clearly register the slightest bite. As can be seen from the diagram, the swan shot leger is a modified form of link leger. The distance between weights and hook should be kept to the minimum, and the float should be attached by the bottom end only and adjusted so that it just cocks nicely on the surface. Accurate plumbing is essential if the tackle is to be set up perfectly. A small shot pinched on to the line directly beneath the float will help to balance the tackle correctly. To stop the line from dragging on the surface, it is advisable to make certain that all the line between float and rod tip sinks. To do this the cast should be made, then the rod tip should be sunk into the water and all the slack line wound in. This will sink the line effectively. Bites are clearly indicated with this kind of tackle, which is well suited to use in large pits.

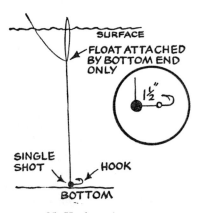

85. Hook on bottom.

The lift method (*see fig. 85*)

This is probably the most popular of tench methods in common use, and although originally devised by the Taylor brothers of Aylesbury for use in local lakes, it is completely adaptable for use in large pits and requires no modification. The secret of the lift method is to have the single swan shot situated no more than 1½ in. from the hook. Once again it is essential to determine the depth of the swim extremely accurately and to set the float so that in use it sits upright directly above the large shot, which should rest right on the bottom. A biting fish will lift this shot up off the bottom, which in turn will cause the float to keel over (see fig. 86). In other words,

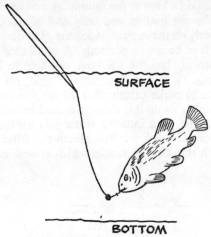

86. Float lifts and keels over as fish picks bait and shot up off the bottom.

the lift method works in reverse to normal float tackle, for instead of the float being pulled under in the conventional fashion, it will rise up and lay flat on the water's surface. The strike should be made as the float heels over. As with the swan shot float leger, the lift float should be attached by the bottom end only. Quills make the best lift floats. This method requires great vigilance, for baits are easily missed if the angler's attention is drawn elsewhere.

Free line fishing

Tench respond well to baits presented on floatless leadless tackle, and for fishing bankside swims, a worm or breadbait fished on this sort of tackle can be most effective. Long casting is out of the question with this tackle for the weight of the bait is seldom heavy enough to cast any distance. Bites on the free line are usually indicated by the line between rod tip and water tightening. A standard bite indicator can also be used.

Legering

Straightforward leger tackle can be employed to good effect when pit fishing, and is often the only practical method to use when attempting to fish likely swims that are situated beyond normal float or free-line casting range. When fishing over a muddy bottom, a normal leger weight has a tendency to sink into the mud and become clogged up. To avoid this, a tube

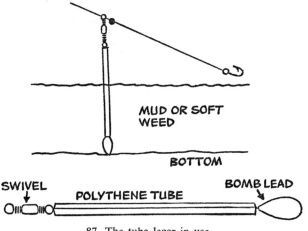

MUD OR SOFT WEED

BOTTOM

SWIVEL   POLYTHENE TUBE   BOMB LEAD

87. The tube leger in use.

leger should be used (see fig. 87). The tube can be made from an empty ball-point refill or standard plastic drinking-straw. The beauty of this type of leger is that even though the lead itself may become buried in mud, the tube usually holds the baited tackle above the mud, and, most important of all, allows the line to run out freely when a fish takes the bait. The tube leger can also be used in thick bottom weed.

Surface fishing

Tench are normally regarded as a bottom-feeding species, but on a number of occasions I have taken tench on margin-fished crust bait intended for carp. Because of my own experiences and also from those of other anglers, I am inclined to believe that tench are more prone to surface feeding than is generally believed. In isolated corner swims, where wind-blown rubbish automatically collects, a small piece of floating bread-crust can sometimes be used to take the odd bigger-than-normal tench. Very little research has been done on this form of fishing, but it seems likely that a floating crust bait could be a winner when big tench are the quarry.

Pre-baiting

Tench are shoal fish which respond well to groundbait. Because of this most knowledgeable tench anglers who are able to visit their favourite waters regularly make a point of pre-baiting their chosen swims for two or three days prior to actually fishing. Bread, bran, mashed potato, sand and rice can all be used to make up groundbait. Ox blood mixed into the basic ingredients adds to the general attractiveness of the groundbait. Ox blood can be obtained from the local abattoir.

Raking a swim

Tench are greatly attracted to muddy water, and before commencing to fish it is often advisable to rake the bottom of the pit thoroughly with a long-handled rake. Obviously this raking disturbs the mud and fills the water with all sorts of edible particles which attract the tench. Strangely enough, although a rake makes a considerable amount of noise and clatter, the fish often move into the disturbed swim within an hour of it being raked. This is difficult to understand for tench are shy fish, quick to take alarm at any bankside vibration. Presumably the oddments of food released by the teeth of the rake help the fish to overcome their fear, for on many occasions I have taken tench from raked swims on my first cast. If the pit bottom is thick with water weed it pays to clear a hole with the rake so that the bait can rest on a clear bottom surrounded by thick weed. Tench find these cleared swims most attractive and sport can be very good when a swim has been dragged in this manner.

Night fishing

Dawn and dusk are normally the best times to catch tench, but night fishing can also be most productive. Free-line fishing in bankside swims is the best method to employ, although it is possible to catch tench on float tackle at night providing a torch is used to illuminate the swim.

11

TROUT

Because few anglers bother to try for trout in gravel pits, it is not generally realised that a good many of these waters contain big trout. Stream-fed pits, for instance, often hold extensive trout stocks, and pits which are subjected to flooding from rivers which are known to contain trout are well worth fishing. Even the tiniest hedgerow stream flowing into a pit can gradually help to stock the pit with wild brown trout, providing, of course, that the stream already contains a natural stock of trout, no matter how small and stunted these fish may be, for once these fish find their way into the deep water of the pit, their growth-rate suddenly accelerates, and instead of attaining a maximum weight of 4 to 6 oz. these fish continue to grow and may exceed 4 or even 6 lb. in weight. A prime example of this sudden growth-rate can be found in the South Cornish china clay pits which are known to hold trout up to approximately 10 lb. in weight. These clay pits are invariably fed by small moorland streams in which the average brown trout weigh at most 4 oz. In times of flood, many of these tiny little trout are washed into the clay pools and begin to grow. 3- and 4-pounders are average fish in these pools, and trout of 7 or 8 lb. are taken during most seasons by local anglers. Nowhere else in Cornwall can trout of this size be found; even the few carefully-stocked reservoirs fail to produce trout even approaching the average-sized clay pit specimens. Do not, however, imagine that these pits are full of monster trout, for they are not. Stocks are limited and the largest fish continually deplete any fresh stocks of small trout by eating them. Consequently only a few of these naturally-introduced fish survive and mature, and catching them can be a problem. In the case of pits which have remained unworked for many years, it may pay to check back and find out whether or not any organised restocking with trout has ever taken place, and if so what sort of trout were introduced and how long before the restocking programme was carried out. Details of this kind can often be found in angling club records or through the owners of the pit in question. If the trout that were introduced were rainbows, then trout fishing will probably be a waste of effort for rainbow trout will seldom breed successfully in this country, and usually die off or disappear within a few years of introduction. If the pit was artificially stocked with brown trout, however, some serious fishing will probably pay off handsomely, for brown trout are hardy fish, quick to acclimatise themselves to almost any conditions, and quite capable of breeding successfully in clean, clear water.

Obviously without consistent restocking programmes, the number of trout present in a pit will decrease as the years go on, but providing the food supply is plentiful the existing fish will continue to put on weight right through their prime years. There are several Kentish gravel and chalk pits which were at one time stocked with trout, and although this stocking took place nearly thirty years ago these waters continue to yield a few big trout each season. Other pits in the Thames and Lee valleys also contain limited stocks of very big trout, as do pits in the Midlands.

By nature trout are normally insect-eaters, and spend a great deal of time close to the water's surface in search of spent flies. Gravel pit fish, however, do not seem to surface feed in the conventional manner, which is probably one reason why trout can remain in a pit for many years without anyone realising their presence in the water. Occasionally, of course, a trout may rise to the surface or even leap from the water, but unless you are close enough to identify the fish when it does jump, it is very difficult to know whether the disturbance is caused by a trout or a coarse fish, for carp, particularly wild, fully-scaled carp, are very fond of leaping high out of the water, and roach or rudd will also jump on occasions.

The trout fishing methods described in this chapter are those designed to catch wild trout from waters where few trout exist. By trout fishing standards they may not appear to be very sporting tactics to use against a game fish. I make no apology, however, to any fly-fishing purist, for the only fly that could be used to take the trout I describe are those designed to look like small fish, and even these would be far from successful, as most big trout are bottom-feeders and scavengers, more prone to take a static bait than a moving one. There are, of course, plenty of well-keepered, heavily-stocked gravel pits which are used only for trout fishing. Waters of this type are often well beyond the financial range of the average angler, and have no valid place in a book of this type. The trout in this chapter are true wild fish of high average size which live in gravel pits all over the country, fish which are few and far between, but which present an interesting challenge to the gravel pit angler who wishes to add a little interest to his general angling expeditions by catching a few game fish.

Big trout are generally most active after dark, and any angler seriously intending to trout-fish is well advised to arrive at the waterside an hour or so before twilight and fish on well into the night. Big trout will, of course, feed at all times of the day, and many a specimen has been taken in the middle part of a hot afternoon; but these are the exceptions to the general rule, and should not be taken too seriously, for as darkness falls and the air and water temperatures begin to fall also, trout become food-conscious and begin to hunt actively for sustenance.

FEEDING HABITS OF TROUT

Pit trout tend to be solitary bottom-feeding fish, rarely rising to the surface in search of food, although when chasing small fish they may pursue their quarry right to the top of the water. The smaller trout seem to feed to a great extent on freshwater shrimps, nymphs and the larvae of many water-born insects. Because of this, maggots make a good, easily obtainable bait for the smaller fish. The larger trout feed to a great extent on water snails and to a lesser degree on small fish. The water snails are swallowed whole and digested in the normal manner. In pits where water snails are common, it is possible to catch big trout which literally crackle as you handle them. This noise is made by the shells of the newly-swallowed snails grating together under the unaccustomed pressure. Small swan mussels and crayfish may also be taken, although few pits hold crayfish in any numbers. Small fish form an important part of a big trout's food chain, any fish of bait size being taken, including very small trout. Exceptionally large trout probably eat as many fish as pike, and an 8 or 10 lb. specimen could easily catch and swallow fish of 1 lb. or more in weight. Luckily trout of this great size are rarely encountered, although they are probably more common than most people realise. There are several gravel pits in the Darenth Valley in Kent which hold huge trout, and the South Cornish china clay pits hold similar specimens.

BAITS FOR TROUT

Maggots

Maggots used either singly or in large bunches are extremely good trout baits. One of the main advantages of maggot fishing for trout is that, being comparatively cheap to buy and obtainable in large quantities, loose maggots can be used to groundbait a likely-looking trout swim. Unfortunately, for obvious reasons, maggots can not be used in pits which hold large numbers of small coarse fish.

Worms

Trout of all sizes are partial to worm baits, and for all-round pit trout fishing, a lively lobworm or a bunch of redworms make the ideal baits. Trout have a nasty habit of swallowing a worm right down, and to overcome this it is advisable to strike as soon as a bite is detected. Two-hook tackle (see fig.

88. Two-hook tackle. For use with large worm baits.

88) is useful when big earth or lobworms are being used, for these stop the worm from breaking up during casting, and enable a really fast strike to be made, without too much fear of missing the fish in the process.

Livebait

Small live fish make excellent trout baits. Any kind of fish can be used, but minnows are probably the easiest to obtain in quantity and for this reason are the most popular. Gudgeon, loach, bleak, small roach, rudd and perch can all be used successfully, but it is advisable to use the loach and gudgeon on float tackle, for on a leger they usually contrive to wriggle under a stone or some other obstruction, and a hidden bait will catch no fish. The ideal size for a livebait is 3 to 5 in., although when fishing a section of pit suspected to hold a really big trout larger baits can be used to good effect. Pike and perch sometimes make a nuisance of themselves by taking livebaits intended for trout, but this is an unavoidable problem which just has to be accepted.

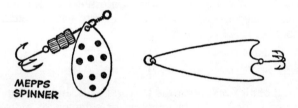

89. Artificial baits for trout. Swedish wobbling spoon.

Deadbaits

Trout, like many predatory fish, are quite willing to pick up and eat small dead fish whenever the opportunity occurs, and because of this habit a deadbait can be used with every confidence for trout fishing. Any small fish can be used for bait, although gudgeon, loach and very small trout are probably the best. River fishermen will all know just how effective a small deadbait can be where big cannibal trout are concerned, and much the same applies to pit trout. Deadbait is best used at night. Unfortunately eels are very fond of fish baits, and if any of these fish are present in the pit, it will not be long before one finds the deadbait. Despite this disadvantage, dead-baits are first-class trout lures and well worth using.

Artificial baits

For the angler who likes to wander from swim to swim in search of fish, spinning is the answer, for trout of all sizes respond well to shiny artificial lures. Small MEPP's Spinners or Swedish wobbling spoons (see fig. 89) are good trout catchers, although almost any spoon with a lively action will take fish. Plug baits and artificial minnows are also quite good, but lack the glitter and movement of the two spoons mentioned. Wobbling spoons should have an overall body length of $1\frac{1}{2}$ to 2 in. This measurement should not include the hook. Choice of colour where baits are concerned depends on per-

90. Spinning flight for use with natural baits.

sonal preference, and experience. A gold or copper-coloured lure often works well in cloudy water, and a silver one seems to be best when the water is really clear. There are no hard and fast rules on this subject, and many anglers buy spoons which are silver on one side and gold or copper on the other.

Natural baits for spinning

Minnows or other shiny bait fish can be mounted on a spinning flight (see fig. 90) and used to take trout. Fresh baits of this type are, however, extremely soft and have a tendency to break up very quickly. Because of this it is sensible to carry a good supply of spare baits, so that a change can be quickly affected when one bait begins to deteriorate.

The kind of trout fishing described in this chapter is far removed from the delicate art of fly fishing normally practised by trout anglers. Long casting with leger or spinning tackle calls for a more robust rod than normally employed, and for obvious reasons fly rods, reels, and lines are useless for trout fishing of this kind. Big trout hooked in deep water are powerful, fast-moving fish, and when choosing a rod for catching trout in gravel pits, it is advisable to bear in mind the kind of hard work the rod will be subjected to. Short rods should be avoided, and unless you intend to devote the entire summer months to trout fishing, it is best to purchase a rod which can be used for other fish as well. A MKIV Avon, either made of split cane or hollow glass, is ideal, for it can be used quite comfortably for perch, big roach, etc. The hollow fibre-glass type is preferable, for it is far lighter than a similar instrument manufactured from split cane, and more important still, will take far more hard work than a split cane rod of similar action. The better-class rod makers will supply rods with a matt varnish finish if requested to do so. This is an excellent idea, for although a glossy rod looks most attractive, it will reflect light badly and this flashiness is usually more than enough to alarm any fish which see it, and trout are no exception to this rule. Hollow glass rods have a softer overall action than their split cane counterparts, but this softness can be an advantage, for it can act as a shock absorber in a time of crisis. A MKIV Avon has a length of 10 ft., which makes it a most useful all-round rod to possess. Longer rods can be used for trout but it is doubtful whether an 11 or 12 ft. rod has any advantage over the 10 ft. rods described.

Reels

A standard fixed-spool reel is all that is required, centre-pins and fly reels being practically useless for this kind of trout fishing.

Lines

Pit trout are by no means line-shy, and there have been numerous cases of really big trout seizing baits attached to really crude sets of terminal tackle. Because of this it is possible to use a fairly substantial b.s. line which can be a great advantage when a big fish has to be stopped practically in its tracks, or held hard in a badly snagged or weeded swim. Even so it does not do to take this to the extreme, and a line of 6 lb. b.s. is quite heavy enough for general trout fishing. A spare reel spool containing a $7\frac{1}{2}$ lb. b.s. line should always be carried, in case an extra-large trout is located, or an average-size fish spotted in a really weedy area. Lines of this strength will not overload the MKIV Avon rod either, and this is an important detail. Monofilament lines are ideal, although it is advisable to pay attention to the colour or finish of a new line. Bright flashy lines should be ignored, as these will probably frighten the fish. Sorrel or blue-coloured lines are best.

Hooks

Almost any kind of freshwater hook can be used to catch trout, although a fine wired round bend hook of the stiletto type is best. The size of the hook used depends on the bait. Maggots or small worms can be fished on size 10 or 12 hooks, large worms on size 4 or 6, and live or deadbaits on size 1 or even 1-0 hooks, depending on the size of fish being used. Treble hooks are unnecessary for trout fishing.

LOCATION OF TROUT

Occasionally trout will show their whereabouts in a water by leaping, or chasing small fry in the shallower water close to the bank. The bigger fish have rather set ways and will often show themselves in this fashion at approximately the same time and place every day. Unfortunately not everyone has the time or the opportunity to be at the waterside day after day waiting for the fish to move and disclose their positions. Consequently it may be necessary to work on a trial and error basis when seeking these fish. The lucky chance angling can, however, be cut to a minimum by concentrating on carefully selected sections of pit which seem likely to hold trout. The mouths of inflowing streams are by far the most likely places to find trout, for these fish love to feel the running water, and know full well that moving water will bring a great deal of food down with it. Where such a stream flows directly into deep water, trout can be fished for at any time of the day, but if the pit is shallow at the point where the stream enters it, late evening or night fishing will yield the best catches. After a period of prolonged warm weather, when most of the pit water is warm and rather stale, these stream-mouth swims are the only places worth fishing, for the trout will collect in these spots to take advantage of the cooler well-oxygenated water. Once again, the fish will feed better at night. Points of land surrounded on two sides by deep water are also likely places to find a trout or two. Very big solitary fish will be found in this type of swim.

Often the bottom of a gravel pit consists of an area of shallow water which extends for anything up to 10 yards from the bank and then drops abruptly away into deep water. Trout will often use a ledge of this type (see fig. 91) as a permanent

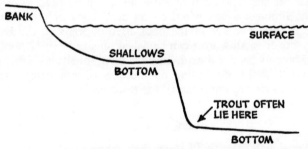

91. Likely trout lie at bottom of a ledge.

base, and a natural bait legered or float-fished over the lip of such a ledge, or a spinner worked along the side of the ledge, will pick up any trout which are in residence. Pit trout do not seem to be greatly attracted to weed beds, although they may well make periodic raids round and through the weed in search of small fry. Fish that do this usually come from some distance to search for food. Sunken tree branches, roots, stumps or other solid obstructions, on the other hand, definitely attract trout, and heavily snagged swims are well worth fishing seriously, for the snags provide the trout with both shelter and food in the shape of water snails which are usually prolific around any submerged timber. When fishing a swim of this kind it is advisable to take the precaution of using heavier line than normal, for any trout that may be hooked will have to be stopped before they can dive into or under the nearest solid obstruction.

Although trout are not shoal fish, a suitable swim may well hold several good fish at a time, and as each is caught and removed, other fish will move in to take the vacant place, because of this it is usually possible to take trout consistently from a single swim, although it is wise to rest the swim at regular intervals. Usually the swims which produce the most fish do not hold the real monster trout, for these extra-big fish appear to be entirely solitary creatures, which live and hunt alone at all times. Their cannibalistic tendencies probably account for this, for any smaller trout which ventured to share the same retreat as a really big trout would soon be eaten.

Strangely enough, very big trout seldom give a spectacular account of themselves when hooked, although they are capable of making extremely long hard runs. The smaller fish, however, often take to the air in a wild display of aerobatics, and can be relied upon to fight to the bitter end. The flesh of these smaller fish is better for eating purposes than that of the big trout which is inclined to be rather coarse in texture. Pit trout which have been feeding on shrimps, crayfish and water snails make wonderful table fish, the flesh being red like that of a sea trout or salmon.

METHODS OF CATCHING TROUT

Float fishing

For daylight work or in swims where for one reason or another the bait has to be kept off the bottom, a float is an indispensable article. Obviously the size of the float depends upon the size of the bait being used, and a float used for livebaiting will be substantially larger than a float used to support a maggot on worm baits. Trout are fast-moving, bold-biting fish and do not seem averse to dragging the largest of floats about behind them. In the Thames, bottle corks are often used as floats by trout specialists who apparently find them to be most successful. Even so, it does not do to take the chance of alarming a fish by using a big float when a small one will suffice, and under most circumstances it is advisable to employ the smallest and lightest float that will support the bait being used. Obviously with large livebaits a reasonably large float will be essential, otherwise the bait will drag it under which will defeat the object of the float. Heavy bob floats (see fig. 92a) were at one time widely used in trout-fishing circles, but these are ungainly awkward floats which create an unnecessary amount

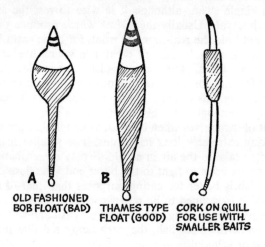

A   B   C

OLD FASHIONED
BOB FLOAT (BAD)   THAMES TYPE   CORK ON QUILL
FLOAT (GOOD)   FOR USE WITH
SMALLER BAITS

92. A: Old fashioned bob float (Bad).   B: Thames type float (Good).
C: Cork on quill for use with smaller baits.

of resistance. Large streamlined floats of the Thames type (see fig. 92b) are far preferable, and very small livebaits can be fished quite easily on large, plain swan quill floats. Smaller cork on quill floats (see fig. 92c) are more suitable for use with smaller baits. Shop-bought floats are usually beautifully finished with varnish. This reflects light and may frighten the fish. A coat of matt green paint applied to the lower half of the float will cure this fault, although it may also spoil the attractive appearance of the float.

Although gravel pits are normally described as still waters, there is in fact quite a lot of water movement and this can be used to great advantage when float fishing for trout, for by finding out in which direction the drift is going it is often possible to cast the tackle out and slowly trot it right through a likely area; ledge swims lend themselves to this sort of fishing. By setting the tackle so that the bait is supported 6 to 12 in. off the bottom, the whole of the ledge can be searched. This sort of fishing requires quite a lot of manual skill, and knowledge of the water being fished. Stream-mouth swims can also be worked in a similar fashion, the flow of water entering the pit being used to 'trot' the float gently along. In very deep, water a sliding float may well be essential (see fig. 93), the rubber stop being set at whatever depth is required.

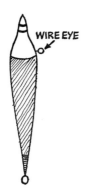

93. Sliding float for deep water work.

Trout are bold biters, and when a fish does take the bait the float will either abruptly disappear beneath the surface, or slide away at ever increasing speed until the fish finally decides to dive, whereupon the float will vanish from view. Both kinds of bite are easy enough to make contact with, and a true strike is seldom necessary. Instead the line should be tightened and the fish will hook itself. A heavy strike at a fast-moving trout may well snap the line, a mistake which could lose the trout of a lifetime. Very occasionally, a light float paternoster will be useful. This method should only be used to fish a livebait close to snags; a free-ranging livebait on standard float tackle would soon work its way into some obstruction which would result in lost tackle and a thoroughly disturbed swim. The float paternoster is designed to keep the bait from roving too far. Great accuracy must be employed when casting the tackle out, for if it overshoots the mark and drops right among the snags on tree roots, then the tackle is bound to become hung up. At the first clear indication of a bite the strike should be made. At the same time the hooked fish should be hustled away from the obstructions and played out in clear water. A trout treated in this fashion is usually too confused to make any serious attempt to regain the safety of the snags, and providing the tackle is sound the fish can usually be netted without too much trouble.

Free-line fishing

For trout fishing at close range, free-line fishing with worm and minnow bait can be highly effective. Obviously neither bait can be cast any great distance without additional weight, and as a lead of any sort defeats the principle of this technique, the free-line method is only suitable for use in bankside swims. The beauty of the free line is that it allows the bait to work and sink in as natural a manner as possible, and because of this it is very useful for fish which show a tendency to ignore a bait presented on leger or float tackle. No extra weight should be employed and the basic tackle consists of rod, reel, line and hook, which makes a very simple outfit to use.

Once the bait is in the water the rod should be held at all times, so that if a fish does take the bait no time is lost before the strike is made. Any delay will lead to deeply hooked fish, which will have to be destroyed. If, of course, all trout caught are going to be killed anyway, this is not quite such an important point, but if the fish is going to be returned then it is absolutely essential to lip-hook it. Bites are registered either by a sudden tightening or slackening of the line. Trout usually take as the bait is sinking and will often ignore the bait once it settles on the pit bed. Because of this it pays to let the bait settle, wait a minute or two to see if a bite will develop, and then work the bait back to the bank by slowly turning the reel

handle and at the same time working the rod tip gently up and
down. Movement attracts trout, and many a good fish can be
taken as the tackle is being retrieved. Once the bait has been
worked right in, a fresh cast can be made and the whole process
repeated until either a fish is hooked, or a move to a new pitch
is called for.

Legering

Trout often respond well to a legered bait, and for fishing
deep holes or other likely places well away from the bank, the
leger is the only practical method to employ. Nothing special
is required in the way of terminal tackle. A plain free-running
leger is quite sufficient. The length of trail between stop shot
and hook depends greatly upon the bait being used; for worm,
the distance is rather immaterial, since trout show little fear
of the lead, and as the worm is not required to move about a
great deal to attract the attention of the trout, a short trail will
be quite adequate. With livebait, the trail should be as long as
possible so that the bait can swim about in a natural manner.
The exception is when fishing close to heavy snags, then a long
trail is out of the question, for it will allow the livebait to seek
the shelter of the obstruction where it will quickly snag the line
in its efforts to hide from view. For fishing in this kind of swim,
a distance of 12 in. is ample, but for more open water a trail
of 4 or more feet should be used. At a time like this the value
of a long rod will become apparent, for a short rod simply is
not long enough to cast a long link leger either easily or
accurately.

Minnows, bleak and small roach make the best livebaits for
this kind of fishing, for all are active fish which will continually
work round well off the bottom. They are also shiny fish, and
as trout hunt a great deal by sight this shininess can be a great
advantage. Gudgeon, loach and perch, although good trout
baits, do not fish well on leger tackle, as they tend to hide
themselves away under stones, or sulk on the bottom.

Big trout, like big pike, will often become scavengers, and a
deadbait can be most effective, particularly where really large
trout are concerned. Small trout make the best deadbaits, but
are not usually very easy to obtain. Any other small fish can
be used quite successfully, however, and a supply of bait-sized

roach, rudd, bleak or gudgeon are usually easy enough to come by. Deadbaiting can be a very slow method but it often produces the biggest fish. As a rule the trout that fall to deadbaits are long, lank black-looking fish, with huge heads and long sharp teeth, true cannibal trout far-removed from the normal run of plump, beautifully-shaped, brightly-spotted fish normally encountered. Big trout in poor condition are best removed from the water, for they are past being good breeding stock and do far more harm than good. Deadbaits can be either threaded on to the line with a baiting needle in the same way as an eel bait (see Eel chapter) or hooked through both lips with a large single hook (see fig. 94). This is a simple easy opera-

94. Deadbait hooked through both lips.

tion, and has much to recommend it, for a bait hooked in this fashion will usually break away from the hook on the strike and will not cushion the power of the strike to any noticeable degree. A threaded deadbait, however, will not break away, and may well 'cushion' the strike so much that the hook will fail to engage and the trout will be lost. Livebaits are best lip-hooked, the hook being inserted through the top lip.

Trout usually take a livebait savagely, but with a static deadbait they have a habit of picking up and dropping the bait several times before moving off with it, because of this it is advisable to wait for a steady run to develop before attempting to strike. The reel pick-up should be left in the open position all the time the bait is in the water, for if a trout does take the bait and run off straight away the line must be free to run out. Any check at this stage will cause the fish to drop the bait.

The twitched deadbait

Originally this was a method used to catch big cannibal

trout in rivers, but it also works well where pit trout are concerned, and for this reason is well worth a mention in this chapter. Trout are very fond of eating stone loach, and for this method of deadbaiting loach make the best baits, although small gudgeon can be used as a substitute if loach are unobtainable. Stone loach are, of course, stream-dwelling fish but they do find their way into gravel pits via feeder streams. A supply of bait-sized stone loach can easily be netted from a stream without much trouble, and half a dozen are easily enough for a night's fishing.

Having first been killed, a bait should then be mounted on a trace consisting of two size 10 or 12 treble hooks and one single hook (see fig. 95). The bait should be mounted so that

95. Miniature deadbait trace for use on trout.

it hangs head down. Very little weight should be used on the line, although a large split shot can be pinched on close to the tail of the bait. This adds a little weight for casting purposes and helps to stop the bait from sliding up the line (see fig. 96).

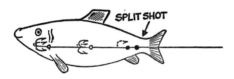

96. Deadbait mounted with single split shot to stop bait sliding back up the line.

The whole object of this technique is to simulate the feeding habits of a live loach as closely as possible. Anyone who has studied loach in the wild state will know that these fish start feeding at the top end of a pool and then drop back downstream a few inches at a time, feeding steadily in this fashion till they reach the bottom or shallow end of the pool. Obviously loach in a pit are less affected by current than loach in a stream, but as these little fish usually gather at a spot directly in front of an inflowing stream, they are still affected to some extent by the moving water. It is not always possible to cast directly up into the mouth of a feeder stream, but the bait can usually be cast across the stream mouth and gently twitched back 3 or 4 in. at a time. By increasing or decreasing the length of the cast the whole area in front of the feeder stream can be thoroughly searched. Trout take a twitched deadbait in a savage fashion, and more often than not hook themselves on one or both small treble hooks in the process.

Late evening or night fishing is best for all natural bait methods of trout fishing, and to avoid frightening any fish which happen to be already in the swim, it is advisable to approach the water as stealthily as possible, preferably in a crouching position, for a dark silhouette is enough to terrify any alert fish that are on the move.

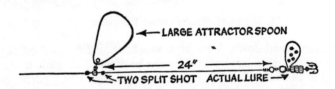

97. Artificial lure used in conjunction with larger attractor spoon.

Spinning

Probably the most practical and lively method of taking big pit trout in broad daylight is to spin for them. Bright, flashy lures are best, and a rapidly retrieved bait is usually more effective than a slowly moving lure. The American and Canadian idea of using a large, hookless attractor spoon set a few feet in front of the true bait can be adapted for use in deep, murky pits where the visibility is bad. This is a simple enough set of tackle which should be made up as follows: first, attach a flashy hookless wobbling spoon to the reel line. Next, tie a 2 ft. length of nylon to the tail ring of this spoon, and at the end of the nylon trail attach the true spinning bait (see fig. 97). The first spoon simply acts as an attractor, and any trout which sees it and comes to investigate the disturbance will probably snap at the small lure as it spins in the path of the attractor spoon.

Playing a big trout

Very big trout usually keep close to the bottom when hooked and, unless the pit is full of snags, the fish can usually be played out without difficulty. The average fish, which normally weigh between 2 and 4 lb., are far more active than the larger fish and often leap in a desperate attempt to shake the hook free. This can be dangerous, for if the fish falls back on to the line a break is almost a certainty. To counteract this problem the rod tip should be lowered every time a trout jumps, then even if the fish does drop back on to the line, it will be sufficiently slack to withstand the shock. At no other time should the rod tip be lowered, and where possible the line should always be kept taut.

12

UNUSUAL PIT FISH

CHUB

Chub, which are normally river fish, are becoming increasingly common in gravel pits that are either stream-fed or situated close to large rivers. Some of the pits in the Thames Valley area hold vast stocks of chub, many of which reach specimen size. On hot days these fish shoal on the surface and can be clearly seen and identified. Strangely enough, chub seem to acclimatise themselves quickly to life in still water, and although I can find no conclusive proof that gravel pit chub spawn successfully, it seems very likely that they do so, for in some pits small chub are commonly caught by anglers fishing for roach or perch. River chub are noted for their shyness, and when transplanted to pits lose none of this caution. If anything, pit chub are even more difficult to tempt than river chub, and those that are caught are usually taken on baits intended for other fish. Carp anglers in particular often take chub on large balls of bread paste, and a specimen chub of $6\frac{1}{2}$ lb. taken several seasons ago from a pit in Kent was caught on a par-boiled potato bait. As yet no one has made a deliberate study of still-water chub, consequently no definite techniques have been developed specifically to take these fish. Chub are handsome brassy fish, easily distinguishable from roach or rudd by their long bodies and large heads. There have, of course, been cases of mistaken identity and more than one angler has landed a fish which he has believed to be a monster roach only to find that in actual fact his 'catch of a lifetime' is simply a medium-sized chub. Mistakes or this kind usually occur because anglers simply do not expect to catch chub from still waters, and when they do land one they naturally assume from its colour that it is a big roach or rudd.

Chub are omnivorous and will eat almost anything that

comes their way. In gravel pits the larvae of aquatic insects and small fish form the bulk of their food, but freshwater mussels, frogs, newts, etc., are also taken. Shoals of chub often gather in isolated corners of a pit and may be found lurking under the rafts of floating industrial rubbish which often gathers in these places. In all probability these fish obtain a lot of their food from amongst this wind-blown debris, for a piece of floating breadcrust fished alongside one of these rafts of muck will often tempt a good fish or two. This crust-fishing technique is exactly the same as the one used for carp fishing, although a lighter rod and line should be used, for chub of all sizes are notoriously line-shy. Large crusts should be used, for even a small chub has a big mouth and prefers a big bait. Legering is another useful technique to use for pit chub, and lobworm or cheese make the best baits. River chub show a great liking for a large knob of cheese, and pit chub seem to share this liking.

Providing they are undisturbed, chub prefer to live and feed close to the bank, particularly where bushes or other plants overhang the water. Because of this it is advisable to leger the bait close to the bank instead of casting it well out into the open water. The best way to fish a known or suspected chub lie is to take up a position 30 or more yards along the bank from the chosen swim and cast the bait along to it. In this way it is easy to fish the swim without unduly alarming its occupants, and any chub which is hooked can be hustled away from the remainder of the shoal without too much disturbance.

Night fishing is equally as productive as daytime fishing, and at night it is often possible to fish directly into a swim without upsetting the fish. On windy days when the water in a pit begins to drift more than usual, float-fishing tactics can be used, for the movement of the water will trot the tackle slowly through the chosen swim. Bread flake or cubes of crust often make the best baits under these circumstances but maggots, worms and cheese can also be used. Big chub will take livebaits quite well and small roach or minnows fished on float or leger tackle can be deadly. These baits normally attract the bigger-than-normal specimens, which owing to their size live a solitary or semi-solitary existence. Because of this it is not advisable to linger too long in any one spot when livebaiting. Instead, it pays to rove from swim to swim in search of fish. Groundbait can sometimes be used to attract big chub, but if used in bulk it may also draw other fish into the swim, and nothing can be more infuriating than to bait a swim carefully for a big chub, only to find that a shoal of small roach, bream or rudd have moved in and are taking full advantage of the groundbait and the hook-bait. Loose pieces of breadcrust floated across a likely chub holt will often bring the fish to the surface where they will give themselves away by making splashy rises at the bread. At these times a small piece of floating crust can be deadly.

Chub can, of course, be caught right through the season, and will often feed extremely well on icy days when other species are reluctant to bite. I remember on one snowy December day taking eleven chub between 3 and 4½ lb. from a small stream-fed pit in Middlesex. All these fish were taken on float tackle and maggot baits from a bankside swim, where chub had been much in evidence during the previous summer. This was an exceptional catch of fish for the water, and nearby roach anglers took nothing, backing up the theory that chub will feed at times when other fish refuse to look at a bait. Whether or not chub of record size can be found in gravel pits is difficult to say, but it seems highly unlikely, although chub up to 6 or 7 lb. most certainly do exist in these waters. Fish of this size are by no means common, but they do exist and are occasionally caught. The average run of pit chub weigh somewhere between 2 and 4 lb. not monsters, but good fish which can provide first-class sport.

As I stated earlier, very little is known about chub fishing in gravel pits, and a great deal of work and research must take place before many of the problems involved are overcome. These pit chub offer a great challenge to individual anglers, or specimen-hunting groups, for skill is required to catch them and only a well-planned campaign will produce consistently good results. For the fly-fishing enthusiast, pit chub offer great scope, for they are active surface feeders and will rise well to a fly. Fly fishing has been a neglected technique where coarse fish are concerned, but there are signs that this interesting method of angling is becoming more popular. On the Continent, of course, fly-fishing techniques are widely used by coarse fishermen and account for big fish of many types.

DACE

Another fish which occasionally occurs in pits is the dace. These, like the chub, find their way into the waters via feeder streams. In some instances clubs have deliberately stocked pits with dace, which have been netted from local rivers or trout streams. Like the chub, these fast-water fish seem to settle down quite well to life in still water, although it is doubtful whether they breed successfully in these unnatural surroundings. Pits which hold large numbers of dace are only infrequently encountered, but I know of several gravel pits in Hampshire, Berkshire, Essex and Norfolk which contain a good head of healthy dace. All these pits are sited close to rivers which hold huge shoals of dace, and many of these fish undoubtedly get washed into the pits when the rivers flood and cover the dividing fields. In fast water, dace are noted for the fast bites they give but in still water I have noticed that the fish tend to suck and pull at the bait rather like rudd. Pit dace are pale-looking fish, easily distinguishable from roach or chub by their slim bodies and lack of colour on the fins. Even on top-quality dace rivers, specimens of 1 lb. or more are rare, and I have no records of any pit dace weighing 1 lb., although one pit near Ringwood in Hampshire has yielded dace of up to 14 oz. These fish are undoubtedly of Avon stock which accounts for their size. On average, pit dace weigh 3 or 4 ozs., and a half-pounder can be regarded as a good one. Above this weight the fish enter the specimen class. No one seriously fishes for dace in pits, and any specimens that are caught are usually regarded as bonus fish. No special tackle or tactics are required to catch pit dace and most of those that are caught are taken by accident usually on maggot bait. Like the chub, dace will rise to an artificial fly, and fly casting can be a pleasant method of taking these delicate little fish.

SMALL FRY

Gudgeon, ruffe, and bleak can all be found in gravel pits, and the gudgeon is particularly common. All these are originally river-dwelling fish which have usually found their way into the pits via the livebait can, or, in some cases, feeder streams. Obviously no one deliberately restocks a water with these small fish, for they offer little sport and are only useful to pike and perch anglers who wish to use them for livebait. All three species mentioned can be caught on light float tackle baited with maggots or fragments of worm. Huge gudgeon inhabit many pits, and I would not be surprised if and when the present gudgeon record is broken it is taken by a gravel pit specimen. Both gudgeon and bleak make excellent livebait, although bleak are rather delicate little fish which die very quickly when used as bait. Ruffe are seldom used as livebait although they are quite good baits. I have caught pike and perch of specimen size on ruffe, and have every confidence in them as fish catchers.

RARE PIT FISH

Very occasionally, rare and unusual fish are taken from gravel pits. These have usually been introduced to the water for experimental purposes, or by private collectors who have decided to clear out their own stock ponds. Ornamental fish often turn up unexpectedly, and large coloured and uncoloured goldfish have been caught frequently by pit fishermen.

One of the most beautiful and spectacular of ornamental fish is the golden tench, or schlei. These are exactly the same shape as the common tench, but are banana-coloured, and marked with occasional dark spots. Schlei were at one time fairly common in ornamental ponds, and have found their way into a few gravel pits as well. Brooklands pit, near Dartford in Kent, holds a limited stock of these beautiful fish and I believe that they can occasionally be caught in the Wraysbury pits, near Staines in Middlesex. I was once fortunate enough to see several of these fish while carp fishing at Brooklands pit, but did not manage to tempt one to take a bait, although one individual specimen weighing, at a guess, $4\frac{1}{2}$ lb. showed interest in a floating crust. Golden tench can now be regarded as extremely rare, and if caught should be returned at once to the water.

Two other foreign fish have created much interest in the

Angling Press during the past few years. These are the Continental pike perch and the American black bass, both of which have been taken from gravel pits in the south of England. A pit near Leighton Buzzard in Bedfordshire was at one time stocked with pike perch, or Zander as they are sometimes called. These fish came originally from the lakes at Woburn Abbey which are noted for the unusual fish they contain. Unfortunately the pit into which these valuable stock fish were liberated was finally filled in by the local council, and the few pike perch that were saved were moved to other waters. The Great Ouse river board also obtained a stock of pike perch which I believe were purchased from a Continental source. Little has been heard of these fish for some years, although small pike perch are now being caught in the Ouse river board area. On the Continent, pike perch reach a weight of over 30 lb., but in this country the largest recorded specimen have seldom reached double figures. Apparently our climate has an adverse effect both on the growth rate and spawning habits of imported pike perch, although I understand that on two occasions the pike perch in the Leighton Buzzard Club waters spawned successfully. Contrary to popular belief, the pike perch is a distinct species, and not a hybrid between the pike and the perch. Although in appearance it has many external features which make it look like a cross between these two common fish, the pike perch is a true predator and has been caught on livebait and deadbait as well as worms, and artificial lures. Pike perch have been caught at all times of the day and night, but there is evidence to suppose that they are basically a nocturnal species.

Small quantities of black bass have been imported into this country on a number of occasions, but, like the pike perch, have never thrived due to our comparatively cold weather. In most instances these stock fish have died out without breeding, and for many years it was supposed that black bass would never reproduce in the wild state, because the coldness of the water rendered the spawn infertile. Then, in 1966, the Angling Press discovered a small club-owned gravel pit in the south of England which had been stocked with black bass long before the last war, and which still produced the occasional catches of small bass, proving conclusively that these fish were successfully reproducing in at least one water in this country. This news created a great deal of interest, for many river boards that at one time had been considering importing black bass into Britain, and had decided against it because of the spawning problems, revised their ideas on this subject, and there is now a possibility that fresh stocks of these fine sporting fish will be imported from America. The black bass is a perch-like fish, very fierce and aggressive, and capable of putting up a tremendous fight when hooked. In America they are caught on artificial lures and flies, but in the pit mentioned, maggot has been the successful bass bait. Obviously a great deal of research must take place before foreign fish can be liberated into our waters, for nature is a funny thing and can unexpectedly run riot. Many of our waters however could do with a decent stock of medium-sized predators, and pike perch and black bass would appear on face value to be ideal, for their slow growth rate and reproduction problems would keep them naturally in check. The final decision for restocking with these fish lies, of course, with the river boards, but I am sure many anglers would welcome the opportunity to add several more fighting fish to the British list.

INDEX